Faith,

MW01595112

Increase Shequria In all her ways!
give her the graces, wisdom, power,
faith, courage, and understanding to deploy

Authentic Worship

God's intention, and how we may be missing it every day.

HeReinz Publishing

REIN JOHNSON

HEIREINA JOHNSON
Hereinz Publishing
California, USA

Dedication

To my family, for your unwavering dedication to my causes, your tireless prayers for me, and your consistent push for me to birth out everything God desires.

To my readers who are dedicated to the discovery of all our Sovereign has for you, I salute you. Thank you for investing in my voice on the matter. May the words on these pages inspire and transform you, and give you the persistence and confidence to deploy.

Table of Contents

INTRODUCTION

Hello, and thank you for stopping here. Whenever I pick up a new book, I admittedly skim through the forewords and introductions to get to the meat and potatoes, highlighter in hand. I've learned though, that often there's some really good and detailed information in these introductions that you actually don't want to miss. So, again, thank you for stopping here, I will not keep you long. I believe there are some preliminary points that need to be made before you dive in.

Why this book?

The simplest answer? It's necessary. The more detailed narrative straight from God's throne is that we have been duped. We have our customs, we have our routines, we have our emotional encounters, we even have powerful encounters, but what is absolutely missing in the earth is what He labeled "authentic worship."

Now listen, we are not talking about authenticity as it relates to well-intentioned hearts to give God glory and praise. I have been privileged to travel the world for ministry and missions, and there is often no shortage of the experience of praise. I see it expressed through song, dance, teaching, preaching, charisma, testimonies, and the list goes on. We know how to come together and manage the religious agendas. In fact, we look for certain elements in the practice of our religious experiences, that when absent, determine whether we perceive ourselves to have had a great experience or a negative one.

So why then would God say that there is an absence of authentic worship? Well, it would be a signal to us that we need to reexamine authenticity and worship and our definitions of them. We will deal with that extensively in this book. For now, let's take a brief look at authenticity.

What is Authenticity

By human definition and philosophy, we learn a couple of things. 1. That authenticity is having the original or the authority. 2. Authenticity is in opposition to that which is false, fictitious, counterfeit, you understand.

Philosophically speaking, authenticity is a human construct. It is the degree to which a person's actions are congruent with their beliefs and values despite external pressures to conformity. A person is said to be authentic when they present by action what their mouth has consistently spoken. To behave contrary to what they promote would make them one who is bad faith in dealing with. An example is a preacher who preaches one thing but does the opposite while expecting others to comply, or a parent that disciplines a child for certain behaviors they consistently model in front of them.

As we try to grasp a description of what manifested authenticity should model in the earth, we run into the dilemma of human nature. One can only be as "authentic" as their understanding of morality, good, bad, etc. Where one might excel in being a great friend to one person and is said to be authentic in that person's opinion, to another they might be a complete failure at authenticity. Human nature gets in the way.

From where are we sourcing our models of authenticity? What establishes our library for what authenticity is? Our perception of that which is good, bad, and maybe even admirable based on what we were taught or experienced. But is that the ceiling or another limitation? If the definition includes being in opposition to that which is false, how do we determine what is false or true? If authenticity avoids the counterfeit, how does one determine what a counterfeit is?

On the surface these may seem like questions that don't require much complex thought, but don't we often find ourselves crushed by unmet expectations? Haven't we predetermined who we would trust based on what they demonstrated? Does their failure to continue to demonstrate or behave within the construct of our expectations make them inauthentic or a counterfeit? Or were they actually authentic, just in a way that proved to be a conflict with our personal values? How could we have measured their authenticity if that definition solely rests on our limited experience of what that is, on our emotions, and preconceived notions? Without a full blueprint of what they were meant to be and where they are along those lines, is it fair to label them inauthentic? *We* certainly don't like to be labeled inauthentic when we are in the process of growth. Indeed, it takes much more than we have given it to understand what authenticity should look like for others and ourselves.

We also use the term interchangeably. We would like to perceive that an authentic person is a good person, but we will also note a person's poor behavior as authentic. As I consider culture, there is a saying often used, "They are keeping it real." This can be stated in praise of "good" preaching, or even when a person proves to be bluntly honest, petty, or a hot head. We will say, "Well, that's them." And that my friend is the problem. When the bar of the standard of authenticity ascends and descends based on what we value, we leave the larger world with a very confused understanding of what authenticity is supposed to model. Our experiences and our learning shape our values, attitudes, perceptions, and actions, which can either prove highly moral or completely disastrous.

I said all that to say, it is impossible to define a human as authentic unless you are completely aware of what the original version of them was supposed to be and how they are measuring up to that. This understanding reveals why we are scattered in our definitions of what makes an authentic worshipper. Even kindness and honesty can be inauthentic. Thus authenticity isn't necessarily defined by words or actions alone. It requires the original blueprint. I cannot determine if a person or thing is producing what it is supposed to be if I don't have the constructor's original intent.

All of us have felt the pressure to conform to something at some point in our lives based on our values, or how intensely we have valued others and what's important to *them*. Society has made numerous suggestions to us about how we are to behave, what we should look like, how much we should weigh, you name it. So how then am I supposed to discover what being my authentic self is when I am presently a conglomeration of a little bit of this and that, right and wrong, in our out, teachings, and sayings? Until we come into full knowledge of whatever the original design of self is meant to be, we are all the sum total of a bunch of moving parts, thoughts, philosophies, and ideas. We are man's dictation instead of God's intention.

I cannot speak for non-spiritual people who were never designed to be spiritual, but assuming that you are a spiritual person or one exploring faith, I can emphatically state to *you*, that our ultimate concern about any and everything we are, should be dictated to us from the throne and not by conforming solely to the world's standards (Romans 12:2). There is a reason

Matthew 6:33 admonishes us to seek first the kingdom (we will explore this in much more detail later). These texts and numerous others are context clues that are drawing our attention to something higher – to a greater understanding about our existence.

When God says, there is too much inauthentic worship, we must seek to understand what both authenticity and worship mean to *Him*, and then take steps to align ourselves with His will. That is what this book attempts to explore and make plain. What are His definitions and how do I ensure I am modeling them?

Forget all you think you know about worship.

This book deals with the definition and demonstration of worship in its entirety, so we will not seek to exhaustively define it here for the sake of avoiding unnecessary repetition, but to really take on worship as God intended, we must uncouple it from our religious experiences. For example, we call services worship services. But do we really worship or just gather for a praise workout, encouragement, and refueling?

The praise and worship leader admonishes us to demonstrate worship and that often translates to us lifting our hands, or some other demonstration such as singing along, speaking in tongues, or praying silently, etc., but that is not worship. All of that is praise and activity, and expressed adoration that leads *to* worship, but it is not what God intended worship itself to be. We would do better to peddle the idea that "God inhabits the praises of His people," to insight demonstrative adoration in the way we expect, rather than to admonish people to worship, and then give them a false illusion of what that even is.

It's a bit of a tightrope walk through here, which will be made so much clearer as we go, but the dictionary definition is even misleading. Worship is defined as *"the feeling or expression of adoration for a deity."* That's not entirely wrong, but without digging deeper into it, we get stuck at evoking a feeling through a consistent set of dictated and learned actions, and we don't become the fullness of what God intended as worship. Demonstrated adoration and lived adoration are two different things. God's definition requires a very specific **lived experience**.

Worship is not a feeling, it's a lifestyle. It's a lifestyle of complete surrender and total obedience to God in accomplishing His intended will for your life. Despite what you heard, there are two wills. There is our will, and there is His will. His will is ultimately "choose ye this day whom you will serve." There is no "permissive" will as if God decides to casually negotiate with us. We may be grateful His mercy keeps us through our shenanigans, but His will remains emphatic and does not waiver. He does not "let us" do anything permissively.

Yes He could intervene, but He has given us a choice. Even when our will is in conflict with His, He is always working to see the Word work as He intended it. He is not permissively sitting by waiting for us to get it together. He is consistent in His attempts to draw the spirit being of us to His throne.

To be permissive is to be habitually or characteristically accepting of or tolerant of something forbidden. When has God ever been that? Don't confuse mercy with permission and permissive. That will be important to hold onto as you read this book as we will get deeper into His will. We step into authentic worship when we surrender our will in exchange for His, no matter the cost.

When you have truly chosen Him as Sovereign, worship comes alive in some exciting ways. **Hold this thought**: Authenticity requires the original intent be made known (in this case His divine intent), and worship is a lifestyle. Worship is not a series of actions that solely produces something out of us by way of praise and its many expressions. Worship— authentic worship-- does produce, but it produces dominion and releases the character and authority of God in the earth. To understand that, we must go back to the beginning, and this will all make sense.

1

.... .Authentic Worship

Part 1
Redefining Worship: Learning worship through Creation

Exploring examples of God's intention and definition of worship through creation.

CHAPTER ONE

So, what were God's Intentions?

"

In the beginning God created the heavens and the earth. The earth was formless and empty, and darkness covered the deep waters. And the spirit of God was hovering over the surface of the waters. Genesis 1:1-2 NLT

To understand where authentic worship begins, we must first understand where God began with it, and more importantly we should reestablish some key things that we must understand about God Himself. Don't worry. I won't bore your patience. Travel with me just a little bit back in time and I promise to make this as engaging as possible.

First question to ponder: Why did God create? Well, I want to answer that with the simplest answer first: because He could and He wanted to. Ok now let's explore that in more detail. He is supreme and He is preeminent. He is a wonder Himself, and every divine initiation from His hand had and yet has an intended purpose in the earth. He just is.

We should not assume that divine creation had anything to do with supposed loneliness. God did not create because He *needed* someone to love. Throughout eternity, our Sovereign is perfect love, and has always known perfect love. He is His own intimate communion with Himself in the God Head-Father, Son, and Holy Spirit. He is the Word with Himself and as Himself, completely fulfilled as Himself with Himself. It is difficult for the human mind to ascertain in some regard because we know intimacy through connection and have most likely never been that self-fulfilled. God; however, has always been completely satisfied. Our creation; therefore, was not a result of some need or limitation within His person.

In the book "Foundations of Grace" by Steven Lawson the sentiments of the creation are recorded brilliantly.

> *In the great expanse of eternity, which stretches behind Genesis 1:1, the universe was unborn and creation existed only in the mind of the great Creator. In His sovereign majesty, God dwelt all alone. We refer to that far distant period before the heavens and the earth were created. There were then no angels to hymn God's praises, no creatures to occupy His notice, no rebels to be brought into subjection. The great God was all-alone amid the awful silence of His own vast universe. But even at that time, if time it can be called, God was sovereign. He might create or not create according to His own good pleasure. He might create this*

way or that way; He might create one world or one million worlds, and who was there to resist His will? He might call into existence one million creatures and place them on absolute equality, endowing them with the same faculties and placing them in the same environment; or, He might create a million creatures, each differing from the others, and possessing nothing in common save their creaturehood, and who was there to challenge His right? If He so pleased, He might call into existence a world so immense that its dimensions were utterly beyond finite computation; and were He so disposed, He might create an organism so small that nothing but the most powerful microscope could reveal its existence to human eyes. It was His sovereign right to create, on the one hand, the exalted seraphim to burn around His throne, and on the other hand, the tiny insect which dies the same hour that it is born. If the mighty God chose to have one vast graduation in His universe, from the loftiest atoms, from macrocosm to microcosm, instead of making everything uniform, who was there to question His sovereign pleasure?

God is all things good and every right and entitlement is simply His. Everything He touched and formed became a magnificent embellishment of His own thoughts. Every detail and every color, every shape and every flower are all some portion of His brilliant mind at work in manifestation, and it was just simply and solely His right.

I remember travelling some time ago to Tahiti. While there I wanted to experience as much as I could, and I took some major risks that changed my perception of Him forever in the most amazing ways. I recall a few events, one of which required me to swim. That was scuba diving. I have played in pools standing safely on the shallow ends, but I have never learned to swim. Where the courage came to scuba dive came from is beyond my understanding all these years later. The trainer promised to teach us the basics, and assured us that being an A1 swimmer was not necessary. On a leap of total "Thou shalt tempt the Lord thy God" faith, I decided to attend the classes and take the plunge, literally.

I will never forget the magnificence of being about 35-40 feet down. As I was engulfed by water that felt like it was standing still to let me pass through its glory, I was in complete and total awe. Coral reefs were as tall as skyscrapers, yet as fragile as baby's breath flowers. All kinds of fish in varieties of colors and shapes swam by me completely unphased by my presence, yet so gorgeous in my view. Fish shaped like trumpets, sponges, spoons, corner stones, and flowers, organisms that looked lifeless until they engaged my touch and shriveled up into their hiding places, and gorgeous turtles were the inhabitants of a world I had never known, and even still were just a small portion of creaturehood beneath earth's surface. We swam for just over an hour gawking over such amazing wonders from rocks that blinked to octopus and starfish casually noting our presence. Everything seemed so aware of us and yet so unbothered by us because everything just belonged. Everything was safe and managed by forces way too big for my human mind to conceive.

As we floated back up to the surface, I was amazed at how I'd spent quite a bit of time in a world I had never visited, seeing things I had never even dreamed of, and yet I was literally still just a few breast strokes from the surface. In all that time and energy spent, I didn't travel even 2 miles. I was looking at one microscopic fraction of a portion of God's imagination, and it floored me.

As I stood on the shore, I remember letting my feet be caressed by the waves, still dazed by what I had encountered. I looked down at sand around my ankles smothering an illustrious hot pink toe nail polish of choice, and I recognized instantly the ocean following its orders to caress the shore only so far before shrinking back in obedient retreat. I understood as I became so aware of how the waters could easily overtake us drowning us all, the divine separation and the control God maintains over it all from the cosmos to the ocean floors.

It was then that I heard, *"You are not common with Me. I am Sovereign."*

We are not common with Him

This may seem like a total digression from the subject, but reverence is an essential and critical part of authentic worship. More and more, as we study the generations, we have lost our fear of Him, which is reverential awe. The emphasis on marveling at His creation is because it draws us to a place of reveling in His glory, His wonder, His creativity, and His sovereignity.

I am not that old, but I remember a time when we maintained an extraordinary respect for the house of God. We refused to enter if we didn't feel it appropriate, we were aware of the mercy extended to us daily, we didn't allow any and everything to take place in the house of the God, and now we are finding more and more ways to be common with society as opposed to living in such a way that draws society to Him, and we do it all in the name of relevance.

We treat God like He is on the same level with us. Reading that might make you say, "No, I don't do that," but how many times have you ignored His voice, or delayed or denied a direct order (assignment) as if He does not know best? How many times have you made decisions on your own when the Word clearly instructs us not to lean on our own understanding but to acknowledge (include) Him in all our ways (decisions and choices)? Our lack of reverence is actually glaring—no blinding. One cannot authentically worship one they do not remain in awe of and in fear of. What you truly worship, you reverence with extreme caution and utmost respect.

So what has caused us to lose this reverence? Apathy. We have spiritually atrophied in many cases because we have become apathetic to the move and presence of God. Apathy is a lack of interest in, or enthusiasm or concern for something. The world presents us with a variety of choices that exclude Him from technology to media to personal pursuit of happiness. We don't bother in many cases to concern ourselves with stretching out in Him. Instead we have our own measures of success and pursuits that we feel are more necessary than He is, short of begging for His endorsement in the moment. We starve Him for attention, but expect Him to move swiftly when we need Him to. He waits patiently for us to even engage the Word, yet we want a Word spoken over us and our situation right now. Most of us would never speak to a person again for much less than the way we treat the one who knows all and is all. We never realize that every battle we choose to have with Him in defiance and disobedience is a fist raised against His throne, His ideas, His omniscience, and His orders. Who are we to defy Him with irreverence?

What keeps us reverential is our attention on Him. When was the last time you stopped and marveled at how grass is growing relentlessly through concrete that God Himself never even authorized (man's "convenience" is often in conflict with God's natural order)? When was the last time you stopped to take in the gentle fragrance of a flower? When was the last time you allowed yourself to stop and thank God for the awesome wonder of pillowy sand or the warm sunshine. When we fail to pay attention to the magnificence of God's creation, we show ingratitude and dishonor. We grieve Him, not just because He cares so deeply for us to even do all this, but because our ignoring it all is actually ignoring Him and so much that we could learn about Him, which would enhance our relationship with Him.

One would be hard pressed to casually and coolly dismiss being dismissed when one has gone out of their way to ensure the comfort and support and love of another. We would be outraged if we extended ourselves in the preparation of celebration of another and they never uttered so much as a thank you or forced a smile. Yet here we are, so consumed by everything but the one who is the Alpha and the Omega. Here we are painfully human marveling anxiously over being single, obsessed with the lack of possessions, engrossed with the need to win man's approval, and inundated with whatever agenda has our attention. Imagine this… our hands trying to work a plan instead of simply revisiting or even inquiring about His original intentions.

This kind of reverence requires relationship, and when that relationship is limited to so called worship services or is only invoked until a need is met, God has become common and we have become apathetic. Be not deceived, even our consistent routine can actually be apathy if the routine is not producing what God intended.

Marveling at His wonders is essentially marveling at Him—reconnecting with our Almighty. There is no way to appreciate His works in a meaningful way without that leading back to appreciating How amazing He is. When you appreciate Him this way, you build confidence and trust in Him, and a willingness to trust Him with your entire being. When He has that kind of dependency on Him from us, He can fill us with more of Himself, and release more of Himself through us in the earth.

I am not suggesting that all of creation was for our sole benefit, He does not need us, but He has graciously allowed us to partake in His imagination and creativity. I cannot speak for you, but I would have never thought of a solar system or a dove. I would have never imagined a giraffe, or a gazelle. Everything seems to give Him praise and honor His will, but us. It often takes extraordinary measures to remind us that we belong to Him, and even when we are focused on that belonging, we are still not producing what we should be. How do I know for certain? That same producing power is not demonstrated in the earth enough for there to be so many believers in existence.

Satan has tampered with our reverence, with our history, with our theology, with our purity of the faith, with the entire truth by introduction of his paganism and rituals. We have gotten away from the essence of time with God and focus on God, much of which has been traded in for entertainment and motivational speaking, We have choked out worship and left only religious activity standing in its place. We offer strange fire by duplicating secularism and offering it up to God as if it is not a stench in His nostrils. Our lack of reverence shows in our social media debates, in our political rants and debacles, in our personal attitudes, and in our lack of thriving, everything competes with God and it shows. It shows God, and it shows the world that we revere God as common and trivial instead of as supreme and the God of Heaven's Armies. The world has no fear of God because often His followers have no reverence for Him. We major in the minutia and make minute what should be glorious. If it were not so, the demonstrations of God would supersede the human and demonic degradation of Him. Fear not, this book is in your hands because God has not left us hopeless. If you breathe in this revelation, pursue, and then execute it, we shall see the glory of God in the earth once more.

So what did God intend?

I want to be clear. Our life in the earth is a necessity today, but God does not "need" any of us. We are His choice,

His means, His tool, and He could have chosen to raise rocks to do His bidding, so we do not relish in our existence as if God cannot operate independently of us, we reverence Him and work in respectful tandem with Him to accomplish *His* will.

Again, none of creation exists because God needed it or felt some sense of overwhelming loneliness. That's simply not the case. Acts 17:24-25 reminds us that He is God who made all things, He does not dwell in temples made by the hands of man, nor is He worshipped by man's hands as if He needs anything from us. It is God who gives us all life, breath, and all things.

In Job 41:11 God checks Job by asking Him, "Who has preceded Me that I should pay him? I own this. Everything under the sun is mine. The same Job was asked in response to his oppressive arrogance, "Where were you when I laid the foundations of the earth and set the stars in the sky (paraphrased)?" Not one of us has ever contributed anything back to God that did not first come from God Himself, so we should not see ourselves as particularly superior or special in this way, but if we have any shine on us, it is because we are operating as one with Him for His good pleasure and purpose, just as all the rest of His creation is. That kind of humility keeps us reverential and consistent in our dialogue with Him about what He requires and expects from us daily.

He created what He wanted. Period. He *wanted* us. He wanted His vision and thought about our being, out of His head and into existence. We are not some meaningless creation because no creation of His is meaningless. We will explore this thought in more detail, but we are a Word out of His mouth and a formation of His hands expected to be his production and His harvest. He is not a disengaged and disinterested Creator. He is an intentional God who deeply loves all the works of His hands and cares us for us with intense and relentless passion.

Our existence is about being an intentional aspect of Him created in the earth to bring Him pleasure and glory. He chose to give Himself to Himself through the creation of humanity as one expression of many. He gave Himself something He could love that would love Him in return. His ruach – His breath – apart of Him was breathed into our form, and we were given the intricate body details that would cause us to procreate and raise our children in love, reverence, and awe of Him—in consistent communion with Him. We would be His people and He would be our God. That was then and yet remains His intention.

In His sovereignity and His own wisdom and His own understanding, He chose our form to govern His earthly creations. He wanted us on earth to run in tandem with His will in Heaven—a mirror of sorts of the constructions of God flowing in their purpose consistently giving Him glory. And still, this same wise uncompromising God made it all our choice without any need on His part to explain.

While I cannot begin to conjecture why that is, and trust me I will not attempt it after all I have said, but who of us wants to have to force anyone to love us?

Oh the power of choice that can either be our greatest achievement or death dealing disaster, but God in His wisdom, holding the end of the story and all its delicious details in His mind has made it so, and it has caused us to have to maneuver back to Him in order to accomplish an end we have only read about in the book of Revelations.

Let's dig a little deeper into what transpired between God's intention and man's decisions. It is important we revisit this at least in brief detail so that we have the full picture of the journey back to authentic worship.

Chapter Reflections

1. Think about God's choice to create. How does it move you? What about it shifts how you see yourself? How you see Him?

2. What are some things that might be different in the earth had Satan not deceived Adam and Eve?

3. Think about your life for a moment. What are some things that you see Satan has deceived you and your bloodline out of. How did his attacks impact your life?

Let's continue on with understanding God's initial intentions.

CHAPTER TWO

Dominion? Dominion! & Thwarted Intention

"

Then God said, "Let us make human beings in our image, to be like us. They will reign over the fish in the sea, the birds in the sky, the livestock, all the wild animals on the earth, and the small animals that scurry along the ground. So God created human beings in His own image. In the image of God He created them. Then God blessed them and said, "Be fruitful and multiply. Fill the earth and govern it. Reign over the fish in the sea, the birds in the sky, and all the animals that scurry along the ground.

Genesis 1:26-28 NLT

Another aspect of God's intention was for us to have dominion. I don't want you to take these things I am saying in this chapter lightly. All of it, if you are paying close attention is defining authentic worship as we go, and it's all very necessary.

Let's define dominion. The dictionary states that dominion is sovereignity or control. That's pretty accurate. God made us mini sovereigns under Him. How cool is that? When we think of this dominion, it's important not to limit it to face value. We may think of it as simply having rule over the fish, the birds, and every crawling thing, but what does that mean? How does one rule over creation and nature? Am I to command dogs to bark or open a pet shelter? Should I stand over the nest of a bird and command it to produce eggs and feed its young? That all sounds pretty asinine right? I mean I owned a pit bull and she had an entire mind of her own. No amount of oil slinging or rebuking was going to make her not behave like a dog. Rescuing her from death I believe was a divine initiation, but that still does not define the rulership that was God-entrusted to us.

> *Then God said, "Let us make human beings in our image, to be like us. They will reign over the fish in the sea, the birds in the sky, the livestock, all the wild animals on the earth, and the small animals that scurry along the ground. So God created human beings in His own image. In the image of God He created them. Then God blessed them and said, "Be fruitful and multiply. Fill the earth and govern it. Reign over the fish in the sea, the birds in the sky, and all the animals that scurry along the ground. Genesis 1:26-28 NLT*

A close look at the text demonstrates first, that God made a decision. He chose to create human beings as we discussed earlier, and here we see that God had dominion, and He chose to give it to us. He gave it back then to Adam. That rulership would eventually be passed down to you and I and every human being placed in the earth by divine will.

Psalm 115:16 (paraphrased) says, "The Heavens are God's, but the earth He has given to the children of men. Dominion is ours, and for us that means that we (believers) have been given the God-given right to make decisions and the authority to rule. Whatsoever we bind on earth shall be bound in heaven, and whatsoever we loose on earth shall be loosed in heaven (Matthew 18:18).

This is a huge responsibility. Hold this thought. It will matter even more later when we discuss deployment. Dominion here is not ownership. We are no more in ownership of the earth as we are our lives. Again, we will get to that, but dominion means *rulership*. God maintains sole ownership, but we are his ambassadors ensuring His will gets carried out.

This is important. We behave as if God is supposed to manage everything that happens in the earth, and we passively pass back the responsibility for dealing with what is out of alignment to Him. That's inappropriate. Our job is to govern and therefore manage what happens here. That does not mean we don't pray or involve God, we must just note that He will not take back an assignment that He has given us. What happens on earth is determined by man not by God, otherwise God lied in giving us the responsibility.

That said; God honors the choices of human beings. He allows free will, as we are not puppets he manipulates for His purpose. Thus, we must all live with the choices that we make.

We often struggle with why so much happens in the earth that is so painful and contrary to the will of God. We throw the onus back on God as if He is the problem. It's reasonable to expect that He can answer the questions we raise, because He can, but God does not make all of the decisions concerning life, contrary to what is popularly believed. We are products and/or victims of whatever humanity has allowed. We were given dominion and with that comes great responsibility.

I don't want to get too far into the next chapter discussing what rulership should look like for us today, but I will say here that many of the things we cannot explain, such as cancers and other deadly diseases are man's inventions or a consequence of them. We talked earlier about concrete and whether God is pleased with it (shameless shout out to my husband for bringing that revelation to my attention), and we must consider how so many of these modern conveniences work against God's natural law and order. Even smog and technological advances can be more harmful than helpful. Man's inventions of medicines and their vast array of side effects have proved more harmful than helpful. Vaccinations that are supposed to help us fight off disease by introducing the disease to our bodies can have long lasting consequences. Birth control and processed foods can be to our detriment. Even the way we vote can have lasting positive or negative affects on human kind and the environment.

We are the sum total of what we have allowed in the name of advancement and "righteous politics." If we don't understand what Adam and Eve had, then we cannot understand what we now have. I have seen far too many believers take a passive approach to rulership because of end time truths. They have essentially become fatalists, and that too is against the divine will of God. Under no circumstances do we leave earth to its fate. We rule by calling things into alignment with the will of God. We can understand that a fate has been decided, but that does not negate our responsibility to affect change as much as possible.

Moses, when He heard God say He would destroy this stiff-necked people, entreated God by asking, "But how does that bring you glory? Won't your enemies say You could not sustain them?" It is not that Moses "negotiated" successfully with God, as if God was undecided and needed coaching, instead what we see here is a heart in perfect alignment that would do what it was destined to—rule. Moses in this case is a profound example of stepping into His authority, and God here does not allow Himself to override man's right to decide His own fate. It is powerful to have that kind of relationship with God where God can even entrust us with His venting. May I know Him that personally.

Moses is not the only example. There are numerous accounts in the Old Testament where the people were destined for judgment but God allowed the prophet or judge to intervene. My point here is that nothing, not even our opinion, should get in the way of our responsibility to rule.

Say this and we will move on. *"God gave me the right to rule, and it is my responsibility to exercise that right in the earth.*

Satan: the thwarter and the thief.

Every time we make a declaration that we will step into essentially anything that God tells us to do, here comes Satan like an annoying spy to thwart our efforts however he can. It's not new though. This started all the way back to the Garden of Eden. We have talked a lot about God's intention, so let's look briefly at what happened as a result of disobedience and draw a direct line for the implications this has on us today, and why we must take seriously our journey to authentic worship. A reinstatement of sorts remains necessary and should be our priority.

I am a parent. Whether you are one or not, I think all of us can relate to either having been instructed on something we ignored, or we have instructed others and they ignored us to a disastrous outcome. I mean; we made it clear. We spoke with authority. We may have even verbally drawn an entire picture or scenario, and still, what was advised was not taken into complete consideration.

My youngest son was blessed to purchase apple air pods. It was something he really wanted, and he used his talents to raise the funds to buy them. These days gadgets are expensive, and I believe air pods at the time of writing this cost around 280.00. For a teenager with no allowance and no job, that can be a hefty amount of money to raise, but in a few short weeks he raised it, and made his purchase.

I will never forget the day he came bursting into my room trying to hold back tears because one of his ear buds managed to make its way down the drain. Our sink is without a stopper, so I completely understood how that happened.

He was so shaken. As a mom I totally felt his anxiety and his pain. I woke his dad and we worked tirelessly trying to disconnect the pipes to recover it. Trust me, the moment didn't come without me fussing at him for being so careless with an expensive product. I knew it was accidental, but he got an earful about having things so small around an open drain. We were unsuccessful at retrieving the air pod, and all I could do was look for the replacement online.

Imagine my total shock when about two weeks later he comes running up to me and falls in my arms completely broken because he dropped the second one down the same drain! How on earth does that happen? We *just* had this conversation. You know there's no stopper in the sink. You were warned about this. In fact, that same day just a few hours before he lost the second one I picked it up off the sink and got on him about leaving it everywhere, *especially* on the sink. So how he managed to lose the second one in the same way was completely beyond my comprehension. We couldn't possibly be having this same conversation again.

Of course he got another mom earful and lecture, because it made no sense to me that after all that hard work and dedication to raise the money, after the devastation of losing the first one, and after us practically tearing the plumbing completely away from the wall, he could be that careless and allow this same thing to happen... twice! I was stern with him, not just because this was careless on his part, but also because as a parent, it hurt my heart to see him lose something that was so precious to him after all he put in to get it. As minor as that example is, if I could feel all that pain and anxiety, and frustration over some air pods that can actually be replaced, how much more has it hurt and offended God that Adam handed over our dominion rights for a bite of fruit, and that we can continue to be almost completely apathetic to reclaiming our position today? How grieved He must have been over the magnitude of the loss and the generational implications! The instructions were so simple, and the warning so clear. How grieved He must yet be when I consider things that He has told so many of us to do that were careless over. I imagine He too must feel like He can't believe He has to have *this* conversation (whatever that is) with us again.

Here is what Moses relates to us about the situation:

> *The Lord God planted a garden eastward in Eden, and there He put the man whom He had formed. And out of the ground the Lord God made every tree grow that is pleasant to the sight and good for food. The tree of life was also in the midst of the garden, and the tree of knowledge of good and evil. Genesis 2:8-9*
>
> *Then the Lord God took the man and put him in the Garden of Eden to tend and keep it. And the Lord God commanded the man saying, "Of every tree of the garden you may freely eat; but of the tree of knowledge of good and evil you shall not eat, for in the day that you eat of it, you shall surely die. Genesis 2:15-17*

Let's take these two passages and walk them backwards. There are some key things we should not miss. First, *"If you eat of the tree of the knowledge of good and evil, you shall surely die."* Hmmm, they didn't actually die. They had children, and pretty much birthed humanity. So what was God saying? Glad you asked! This key intention of God will matter later. I know your hands are full, but hold this one too.

From the moment man was a thought in God's mind, eternal life was a given! God intended for human kind to dwell on the earth forever fulfilling His will to be in relationship with

Him. We inherited without merit or any doings of our own, the gift of life eternal. Age most likely would not have occurred in the way we understand it and how the body breaks down because of it, but who knows. Eternal life was the plan, and a tree of life that they *could* eat from was available to them.

Second, we see *"The Lord God took man and put him in the Garden of Eden to tend and keep it."* This too is another important clue for us to catch. It's very important that when we study the Word we have appropriate exegesis of it. Exegesis is the critical explanation or interpretation of a text, especially of scripture. The bible is not a book. We should not assume that we have automatic understanding of it as it has been translated, and things do get lost in translation. While some texts like, "Thou shalt not kill," seem to be pretty clear, we should not forsake our duty to explanation. There's a reason God said it, and researching that reason gives us way more insight into what life means to God and what it should mean to us. Allow me to stay with this thought briefly about exegesis, as it will come up again.

I remember being in Africa, and I was blessed to be hosted by a leader, his family, and many delegates in that region. After being served my plate, I looked around and noticed I had nothing to wipe my hands. Casually and politely I asked one of the hosts for a napkin. The guests and dignitaries at the table erupted in laughter. Completely clueless, I looked at the host and asked what I had missed. She explained that in their language a napkin is a diaper. I was flabbergasted. In the middle of a meal in front of all those important people I declared out loud that I needed a diaper. Can you imagine the assumption on their part? How utterly embarrassing it was.

Now, imagine that word napkin used in the Bible and my reading it and their reading it. It would yield two completely different understandings of the text! Whoa!

How many times have you heard at a funeral, "Blessed are those that mourn, for they shall be comforted?" That sounds right. It's the absolute truth. God does comfort. And at face value in a moment when I am broken by the loss of a loved one, that seems to make absolute sense. There is no lie in it. However, it's not at all what Jesus had on His mind when he preached that day.

The statement is a part of a larger sermon that should not be taken out of context. Jesus was baffled by the rejection of Him by His own people. He was outraged by the desecration of the temple, and He was very clear of what His purpose in the earth was. Instead of angry silence, He takes a topic and begins to rebuke and instruct. He starts His sermon (Matthew 5:3) with a promise that the Kingdom of Heaven belongs only to those who recognize their poverty *of spirit* and thus repent and *believe* the gospel. We will define repentance shortly. As He gets to Matthew 5:4, He is speaking to a different kind of mourning. This kind of mourning speaks to one's realization of moral failure and the deep conviction that follows. We literally begin to mourn for (because of) our sin and offenses, but, as we come to this place, there is the promise that repentance (a complete turn toward faith and obedience) will assure us eternal life. In other words, we are not bound to shame and condemnation. God honors our shift and matches it with destiny! How amazing is that understanding? It's an entirely new world and word of hope. To think we limited that understanding to you will eventually be comforted through your grief of the loss of a loved one. Both versions matter, and God uses the same texts to make different points as He pleases, but which is more impactful in light of destiny? We must have appropriate context.

Appropriate context comes through revelation and study. The Old Testament readers would have been written to in Hebrew. The New Testament readers would have largely been spoken to in Greek. Either way, every text merits deep study, even when you think you understand it. Key words translated to English do not always mean what we think. We must take key words and translate them back to the original language it was written in to get the full point as I demonstrated above.

I promise this was not a pointless digression. As you move forward into walking into authentic worship, you will need the Word. The Presence and the Word are one. In order to understand what God is speaking to us through it, you need the tools for how to interpret it.

Now, let's revisit the text: "*The Lord God took man and put him in the Garden of Eden to **tend** and **keep** it.*" I can't speak for everyone, but I can speak for myself and admit I have heard the interpretations of this text, and almost all of us assumed "tend" and "keep" meant grounds keeping. Many of us assumed Adam had to be gardener. That's not quite right, because we read a little further down in chapter 3 verse 23 that when Adam was banished, one of the curses he inherited for his disobedience was having to work the ground from which He had been taken. So what exactly was Adams charge? What was tending and keeping?

In Hebrew, the word "tend," meant supervise, control, oversee, or superintend, to look after or look out for. That's so important! We will get to that in just one second. The Hebrew definition of the word "keep" is to retain, to preserve, to guard, and to forever own. Adam's assignment was essentially to maintain God's orders or will and look out for anything that might hinder his ability to retain or maintain ownership of what was given to him by the obstruction of that will. In other words, "Adam I am placing you here, keep it guarded from anything that might altar my plan or seize what I gave you."

So, what did God know that Adam didn't? Obviously, God had the knowledge of good and evil. We know this because He demonstrated this truth by forging a tree. But in a literal perfect world, why would Adam need to be given the instruction to tend and to keep what was already promised unless there was some outside force or something lurking that could pose a threat to the promise. Further, why would God not just say, "Hey, by the way, watch out for Satan, he will try you," and why would God even create a tree that would serve as a possible temptation?

We've established that God could just because He felt like it, and that stands. We also come back to the power of choice. God in His infinite wisdom offered us choice, always. He took a risk that He understood would be the difference between routine and authentic worship.

Remember, God didn't' create a bunch of robots that would do any and everything He said. He created us in His image. That means with His characteristics. and His ideas. The ability to choose between right and wrong is the line that separates us from being human or mindless slaves. He created us out of His love for us, in hopes that we would choose in return to demonstrate that same love back to Him. He did not program us. He gave us autonomy.

What good is it to have the power to choose if there is nothing to choose from? How does that right get exercised? It is risky on the part of God but is necessary nonetheless. If there is only ever one road, then man has no choice to make. When another road is introduced, therein lies the mystery, adventure, and power of choice. That said, we were created with the ability to choose between right and wrong, but having that ability would be meaningless if there was no introduction to wrongdoing.

By providing man with the tree of life and the tree of knowledge of good and evil, God was honoring His word to give man rulership, freedom, and autonomy. God was providing man with the right to choose to obey, to choose to do good, or to choose to disobey and choose to do evil. God would not be true to His word if He had not, even knowing man would choose wrong.

How many of us have ever been given license and freedom to accomplish something only to be micromanaged and told how to do it later? It's frustrating and even demeaning right? Your first thought is often, either you are going to let me do this my way, or you take it back. God would not make a promise to let us rule and then tell us how to do it. He is available for consultation, but He will not relent on a promise. What is so amazing about God, who knows all, is that a mercy and redemption clause is always built in to a promise. There is always in His kindness a way of escape and a path back to Him. He is truly good!

So let's talk about this snake or this force that was present. How did it get there or where did it come from? How was it able to slither into Eden and disrupt God's initial intentions?

Again, one might ponder why God would create something so horrid as Satan (also known as the devil), but that question is based on flawed reasoning since it assumes that we have the right to critique God. However, in an attempt to address said flawed reasoning, God did not create Satan (or the devil), as we know him. Genesis 1:31 tells us that God examined it and declared it was good. **God...examined**. Do we need to say more? We spent a few pages talking about Him and the awesome wonders and works of His hands. It is doubtful that we need to examine His examination. If He said it was good, it **was**. Period.

Still, by the time we arrive at Genesis chapter 3, something has transpired. We find that Satan in the form of a serpent was tempting Eve to sin. The canonized Bible we carry does not cover all things in chronological order, and there are books that are mentioned in our Bible that are authentic but not included. We don't get from our Bible the depiction of heavenly creation as in non-canonical books, but from it we can derive that angelic beings existed (as we see them throughout scripture), and it is obvious that there was an angelic rebellion led by Satan. That knowledge also indicates that angelic beings were given the same freedom of choice as man—to choose God. If that is not a picture of Kingdom and "Thy will be done on earth as it is in Heaven" I don't' know what is.

The Bible gives us this information about Satan.

"You were the model of perfection, full of wisdom and perfect in beauty. You were in Eden, the garden of God...You were anointed as a guardian cherub, for so I ordained you. You were on the holy mount of God; you walked among the fiery stones. You were blameless in your ways from the day you were created till wickedness was found in you. Through your widespread trade you were filled with violence, and you sinned. So I drove you in

disgrace from the mount of God, and I expelled you, O guardian cherub, from among the fiery stones. Your heart became proud on account of your beauty, and you corrupted your wisdom because of your splendor. So I threw you to earth; I made a spectacle of you before kings" (Ezekiel 28:12–17 NIV).

Cherubim are depicted in Scripture as powerful and majestic angelic creatures who surround God's throne. And Lucifer had once been a guardian cherub. Ironically, after Adam and Eve succumbed to the devil's temptations, disobeyed God, and were expelled from Eden, God sent cherubim to guard Eden (Genesis 3:24).

What caused Satan's fall? A proud heart borne of his obsession with himself. He allowed his perfection to be his corruption. I want you to note the similarities between Satan and Adam. Lucifer was *anointed* a guardian cherub. To be anointed is not just to be slathered with oil. It is, catch this, you will need this later, to have a divine or holy office conferred upon you, in this case by God. Satan and Adam had the same job – tend and keep! Satan got tripped up by his own pride, which caused him to rebel, and like the bitter rival he is, He made sure to trip up Adam from his most vulnerable place. Today, he is still on that same agenda with you and I—keep them from dominion and destiny by finding and infiltrating their vulnerable places. What a Jerk!

Satan was not satisfied with just worshipping God; he wanted to *be* God. Once a beautiful and powerful angel, he lost his former exalted position in heaven because of his lust, and he tried and tries to destroy man, beginning with Adam, with that same lustful spirit.

> "How you are fallen from Heaven, O Lucifer, son of the morning! How you are cut down to the ground, you who weakened the nations! For you have said in your heart: 'I will ascend into Heaven, I will exalt my throne above the stars of God; I will also sit on the mount of the congregation on the farthest sides of the north; I will ascend above the heights of the clouds, I will be like the Most High.' Yet you shall be brought down to Sheol, to the lowest depths of the Pit" (Isaiah 14:12–15).

Lucifer ("star of the morning") became Satan ("accuser") when he fell to the earth. Jesus, speaking of this event, said, "I saw Satan fall like lightning from Heaven" (Luke 10:18). When Satan fell, he did not fall alone. Scripture tells us that he took one-third of the angels (see Revelation 12:4). Considering that the angelic host numbers more than 10,000 x 10,000 (see Revelation 5:11), that is a sizable group. They account for the fallen angels, or demons, that now do his bidding. As a result, Satan is a fallen, spirit-being with a well-organized network of demon powers to help him accomplish his purposes. Those purposes, according to Jesus, are to "steal, kill, and destroy" (John 10:10).

That's the bad news. The good news is that two-thirds of the angels are on our side! As the prophet Elisha said to his servant, "Don't be afraid. Those who are with us are more than those who are with them" (2 Kings 6:16).

So what did Satan steal? One thing he stole from Adam was what he himself lost when he lost his exalted position—guardianship. We can also note guardianship as dominion. The same consequence that fell on Satan—expulsion from heaven is the same consequence for disobedience that fell on Adam—expulsion from the Garden of Eden and a stripping of that authority.

Expulsion, be it Satan being expelled from heaven or Adam and Eve being expelled from the garden, meant being ushered out of the presence of God as well. Satan's deception cost man to some extent relationship with God. As we read further in Genesis and ultimately all throughout the Bible, it's pretty clear that God didn't completely reject man, but something did shift, and it's important to note as we wrestle with the notion of what authentic worship really is. When we consider what it takes to get into the presence of God (and we will cover this in much more detail later), we note that it requires an intentional focus. Though God is everywhere, we often are not as cognizant of that fact and assume then that we must evoke Him for a visitation. Again, this will be looked at in depth.

Adam woke up with God, walked with God, and communed with God all day everyday. Being in the presence of God was commonplace. There was no need to reach up for it or turn attention to it per se, because it just was. Adam had the privilege of living with God literally.

Why is that a big deal? Not only was it God's intention, it had certain inevitable consequences. Think about growing up living with those that you did, You knew their voice, you were exposed to the real them beyond whatever they portrayed outside of the house, you were shaped by whatever experiences you had with them positively and maybe even negatively. It is said we are a product of our environment. What we learn about life, we ultimately learn from the experience of our dwelling place.

My mother was very strict growing up, and discipline was common. As a child I had my own understanding of what I thought was necessary and unnecessary. I sometimes judged her methods and decided that as an adult and parent I would do things quite differently. Ironically, as I became an adult and a parent, I found myself sounding just like her. It would often amaze me given I was so determined to be my own person. Still, I found myself heavily influenced by her and my grandmother. My children watching me determined they would do things differently than I did, only to discover that they too could not escape the "dreaded" sounding just like their mom.

Imagine what living in the presence of God would have been like with a daily attention to it because it just was. What might it have been like for God to be our literal dwelling place? God's intention was also perfect fellowship. As He gave Adam the charge to be fruitful and multiply, his children would have been birthed right into the presence of God, and as a result, they would grow up knowing Him intimately. Just as I was a bit of a replication of my mother, and my children grew to be a bit of replication of me, humanity birthed into God's intention of perfect relationship would be replicas of His character, power, love, and authority in the earth.

Satan's deception snatched all of us out of that birthright. He stole relationship and dominion and set up his false kingdom in the earth.

Satan desires still to be worshipped. Expulsion did not quench his thirst to be God. We see today that Satan has complete attention on him in almost every aspect of life. God wanted perfect relationship through daily communion and guardianship, and on earth we see that there is gross neglect, even in the church, of genuine relationship with God that reproduces God in the earth in an awe-inspiring way. Satan is worshipped in the media, in entertainment, in symbolism, in education, in government, in the family structure, in religion, and in big business. It remains our job to snatch back the authority.

The third thing Satan stole was our right to the gift of eternal life. God's plan was to have the creation of man dwell with Him forever. Man had the tree of life and would not know death, as we understand it. God warned Adam that if he ate of the tree of knowledge of good and evil he would surely die. Adam may or may not have had a clear concept of death when the instruction was given, because things like death and sickness did not exist until he fell. It was present as an option, but he would not have ever known it had he obeyed.

Satan's deception caused God to recess the tree of life, because it was not God's intention for man to live forever in the state of sin. When Adam fell, a life span was given to man, and eternal life and eternal fellowship with God would have to be restored another way.

Another thing Satan stole from us was our sight. Genesis 1:26 records God saying, "Let us make man in our image, after our likeness. This is important. We were made in the image of God! What does that mean? Glad you asked. The use of the word image in this passage means "in the likeness of that which is in Heaven." God Himself is the blueprint for our being. We are a replica. We were meant to be a literal reflection of Him – His character, His nature, and His dominion.

Satan was so obsessed with His image that it caused his expulsion from Heaven. His deception would cause us to not perceive ourselves as in the image of God. When man fell, we lost the ability to see ourselves as God sees us. Satan is heavily invested in keeping us from that to this day. It opens up too much that becomes a threat to him.

We said earlier that worship is allegiance and obedience. When we ignore God, lose focus, or are enticed away from the obedience that belongs to God, we place our worship upon Satan, and he is a cunning lure. When Adam, the guardian, bit that fruit, he handed Satan the keys to the kingdom and transferred ownership of the earth to him. He also forfeit the presence of God in the way God intended, which would make our understanding of God today, extraordinarily limited, and he doomed us to a life span limit. It was indeed a devastating blow to the kingdom of Heaven, but not one that caught God by surprise, be clear. Adam was the guardian—the original keeper of keys so to speak. His disobedience lodged those symbolic keys from his hands and placed them with Satan who earned his "kingdom" by deception, and the world is worshipping him daily.

We, post Christ, are to be the keepers of the keys, meant to restore relationship. See more about this in chapter 4. We are the true and rightfully entitled owners of this land, and Satan will not give up or relinquish his hold silently or easily. What we must note from this understanding is that we are here to reestablish our God-given authority in the earth, and we, as God did before us, are to boot Satan from it in every way possible. His place is in hell. We understand that a set time for him is established, but that does not negate our responsibility to continuing in the expansion of kingdom by putting God on display as we yield to Him and obey Him above all.

When we fail at complete obedience, we too relinquish the keys back into the hands of Satan. I cannot speak for everyone, but after His violent and disgusting interruptions into my life, I am not willing to continue to allow him free reign.

Chapter Reflections

1. What are the key things Satan stole thanks to the fall of man?

2. From this chapter we learn that Satan dominates us in every area of life on earth. We briefly categorized those areas above. When you consider them, what area captures your concern and attention the most? That may be your mountain to conquer. It's ok to be drawn to more than one. Pray for specifics regarding your purpose in the earth. We will revisit this.

CHAPTER THREE

Dominion Today, and Our Apathetic Nature

> "
>
> I, the LORD have called you to demonstrate my righteousness. I will take you by the hand and guard you, and I will give you to My people, Israel as a symbol of my covenant with them. And you will be a light to guide the nations. You will open the eyes of the blind. You will free the captives from prison, releasing those who sit in dark dungeons. Isaiah 42:6-7

We will spend time in the coming chapters dealing with authentic worship and dominion as deployment, so we won't get too in depth on that here, but I want to call your attention back to some things that said earlier to build the case again with you that we must address our own spiritual apathy. There has been and remains a direct satanic attack on our relationship with God. We will talk more about the role of Jesus in chapter 4 and how that all relates to us, but I will state this here as well: Jesus did not come to establish a religion. He came to introduce us to kingdom and restore us back to perfect relationship with the Father, just as He had. Man created religion.

Before you cast the book away and label me a heretic, let me be clear. Religion is not a bad thing in and of itself in the purest sense. I am called to the mountain of religion, so I am certainly not saying toss the idea of it. There must; however, be a shift within it that moves it from religious ritual to actual kingdom expansion and citizenship. If within our religious constructs we do not honor the one true and living God as Sovereign, and if we are not having the conversations God desires, it is all merely an exercise and gathering for spirituality, not kingdom. Our existence—this notion of rulership—is ultimately to restore as much of mankind back to God and kingdom as possible. Despite all Satan is doing, that is our job. In order to do that job, we must address all forms of spiritual apathy personally and globally. The conversation about or role in the earth must start here before we can ever consider operation in authentic worship. We must address the apathy before we get to strategy.

Address the Apathy - The Death of Awe

In earlier chapters we discussed apathy and defined it as lack of interest, enthusiasm or concern. We talked at length about the wonders of God's creations and how avoiding the time to experience His creativity and appreciate it in all forms leads ultimately to taking Him for granted and to irreverence. It is said that familiarity breeds contempt, and I have found that to be true. That which we are spoiled to see at all times is often the thing we begin to neglect or dismiss. I believe everything God created deserves our consistent attention —not as worship but because it draws us (or should draw us) back into the worship of *Him*.

Are we so routine driven that we have lost the awe of God? There used to be a time that we would anxiously await gathering together in fellowship with believers in great expectation of an encounter. It was in those awe filled moments that God could move extraordinarily and perform in ways we could not articulate if we tried.

Paul Tripp articulated it brilliantly in *"When you lose awe for God,"* when he wrote:

"Truly God is good to Israel . . . " (Psalm 73:1).

I don't think we have categories that get at what these words are saying. Pastor, these words can roll off your tongue so easily your mind barely has time to consider their content. The danger is that these words have become so familiar and mundane that they barely draw interest out of us, let alone awe. At breakfast you'll say something like, "Wow, this cereal is good!" Or, "We had a good time at the park." Or, "Let me tell you where to get a good cup of coffee." Or, "Sam is really a good intern." So maybe when we read that God is good, the worship transaction that's supposed to happen inside us doesn't happen anymore.

When you read the words "God is good," your heart should be filled with wonder, gratitude, humility, and love and this amazement should fuel your ministry. Or to capture what our response should be in one word: AWE. Now, this is where the problem lies: I'm convinced that many of us live and do ministry day after day without any awe whatsoever. We live days, maybe even weeks, without wonder and amazement even in gospel ministry. What should stun us doesn't stun us anymore. What should leave us in silent, amazed worship has become so familiar it barely gets our attention in the clutter of all the other things in ministry that command our attention. We walk through our daily ministries without an overwhelming sense of gratitude. We don't notice the glory displayed all around us that points us to the one glory that is truly glorious: the glory of God. No, we see:

- *the worship leader who thinks he's the senior pastor*
- *the mission conference details to be planned*
- *competitive ministry leaders who are fighting once again*
- *the intern who's messed up*
- *the hard elder*
- *too much traffic*
- *another long meeting to attend*
- *the car that needs repair*
- *the movie we have to see*

- *the blogs we can't live without*
- *the cool restaurant we can't wait to visit*
- *the sabbatical around the corner*
- *the deacon who is mad once again*
- *the busy holiday season that quickly approaches*
- *the garage that is too full to house the car anymore*
- *the perennial financial problems at church*
- *the weight we didn't mean to gain*
- *the ministry dreams that are slipping through our fingers.*

For sinners, the road between awe and complaining is very short. You and I were created to live our lives in the shadow of awe. Every word we speak, every action we take, every decision we make, and every desire we entertain was meant to be colored by awe. We were meant to live and minister with eyes gazing upward and outward. We were meant to live with hearts that are searching, hungry, seeking satisfaction, and being satisfied. Bad things happen when pastors lose their sense of awe. Bad things happen in ministry when we've no wonder inside us. Bad things happen in local church leadership when we're no longer amazed. Bad things happen when we look around and nothing impresses us anymore.

Sin, which is essentially anything that gets in the way of our relationship with, our personal reverence for, and our complete obedience to God, robs us of that sense of divine wonder meant to shape our lives.

Satan keeps us easily distracted by what the world thinks is best or palatable, and we must work tirelessly to train our brain to not give in to being conformed to the customs of this world. Apathy usually begins subtly and then advances into a full on vision and pursuit opposite of what God desires for us. Our own understanding gets in the way constantly because we have made worship familiar and, as stated earlier, only religious activity is left standing.

I remember God saying to me, "If I completely removed my presence, 99.9% of what they (the churches) are doing would continue, and I would hardly be missed. That hurt. But I have found it to be true as we invoke God to have His way and then won't wait for Him to. We can't sit in awkward silence or just sit before God to hear. We have followed the pattern of having to have the band and the best praise teams, and the recording artist praise and worship leaders, and all the things needed to put on a good show, and we have lost the essence of coming into the sanctuary and just being in awe of God. I am not saying these things are bad, enhancements help, but if the help never draws us to an awe of God and an encounter, it is no help at all.

I said earlier, we are not common with Him. He is Sovereign. When we fail to see Him as that, we fail to be impressed. When we fail to be impressed, we fail to serve. That is exactly what the enemy wants.

Address the Apathy – The Death of Reverence

One can only be as reverential as one is awe struck. Thus, we must manage what our own ideas of success are. In Exodus, there is a magnificent tale of a great rescue of the Children of Israel out of the hands of Pharaoh. It's an exciting tale of Moses, his staff, miracles, a consistent demand to let the people go and God's more and more intense response to Pharaoh's rebellion. It's fascinating quite literally. The Children of Israel watching on were most likely quite awe struck in the moment. I would have been. I imagine that seeing God move this way, so dramatically, threw them into reverential fear.

We also see that after a dramatic escape, there is a constant whining and complaining to the extent that an entire generation had to die out before they could reach the Promised Land. Nobody wanted to sacrifice anything for their newfound freedom. As much as they saw God do, their reverence was temporary and dependent upon one great exploit after another. What they had for God was respect and not reverence and that is what we see in the church today. The two are used interchangeably but they are not the same. While respect is a special regard, or consideration for, reverence rises to a higher level such as worship, adoration, awe, veneration, or devotion.

As the church has become cultural captive to the humanistic demands of the world, it has absorbed a perverted understanding of spirituality as it seeks to adapt to culture instead of calling culture into the adaptation of God. We thirst for popularity initially stating that we want to reach more people for God, but often become captivated by the benefits, and we see those benefits such as the seed lusted after and lied after and manipulated after all the time. We have become obsessed even with power so much so that we take no notice that we are conjuring and soothe saying instead of authentically operating in authority and prophesying as a clean pipeline.

Much like the children of Israel and their incessant reliance on and lust for the look of Egypt (their former oppressor by the way), we are looking to mega movements and big names to define our success instead of to God's divine propulsion. When we shift our attention away from the process that leads us into reverence, we become overly enticed by man's vision and Satan's luring, and we become something God never intended. Just look at the state of affairs. Pastors are spewing hate speech from the pulpit, they are cursing in the pulpit; we see scandal after scandal, and more reality show behavior than we see God. A thirst for anything other than Him places our roots in lust, pride, and invention. We will literally start creating the life we think we need to have juxtaposed to seeking the one God intended. A shift a way from reverence and introduction to disobedience has dangerous consequences. The church is supposed to be a beacon, but we have seen a dark shadow cast on it for decades, because our routines and agendas must be strictly adhered to. It makes no sense.

I want to draw your attention to the book of Ezekiel the 8th chapter:

> Then on September 17, during the sixth year of King Jehoiachin's captivity, while the leaders of Judah were in my home, the Sovereign LORD took hold of me. ²I saw a figure that appeared to be a man. From what appeared to be his waist down, he looked like a burning flame. From the waist up he looked like gleaming amber. ³He reached out what seemed to be a hand and took me by the hair. Then the Spirit lifted me up into the sky and transported me to Jerusalem in a vision from God. I was taken to the north gate of the inner courtyard of the Temple, where there is a large idol that has made the LORD very jealous. ⁴Suddenly, the glory of the God of Israel was there, just as I had seen it before in the valley.

> Then the LORD said to me, "Son of man, look toward the north." So I looked, and there to the north, beside the entrance to the gate near the altar, stood the idol that had made the LORD so jealous.

> "Son of man," he said, "do you see what they are doing? Do you see the detestable sins the people of Israel are committing to drive me from my Temple? But come, and

you will see even more detestable sins than these!" Then he brought me to the door of the Temple courtyard, where I could see a hole in the wall. ^{8}He said to me, "Now, son of man, dig into the wall." So I dug into the wall and found a hidden doorway.

"Go in," he said, "and see the wicked and detestable sins they are committing in there!" So I went in and saw the walls covered with engravings of all kinds of crawling animals and detestable creatures. I also saw the various idols worshiped by the people of Israel. Seventy leaders of Israel were standing there with Jaazaniah son of Shaphan in the center. Each of them held an incense burner, from which a cloud of incense rose above their heads.

Then the LORD said to me, "Son of man, have you seen what the leaders of Israel are doing with their idols in dark rooms? They are saying, 'The LORD doesn't see us; he has deserted our land!" Then the LORD added, "Come, and I will show you even more detestable sins than these!"

He brought me to the north gate of the LORD's Temple, and some women were sitting there, weeping for the god Tammuz. "Have you seen this?" he asked. "But I will show you even more detestable sins than these!"

Then he brought me into the inner courtyard of the LORD's Temple. At the entrance to the sanctuary, between the entry room and the bronze altar, there were about twenty-five men with their backs to the sanctuary of the LORD. They were facing east, bowing low to the ground, worshiping the sun!

"Have you seen this, son of man?" he asked. "Is it nothing to the people of Judah that they commit these detestable sins, leading the whole nation into violence, thumbing their noses at me, and provoking my anger? Therefore, I will respond in fury. I will neither pity nor spare them. And though they cry for mercy, I will not listen."

It's difficult to read this passage and not feel some form of remorse. It's difficult to read this and not feel for them some sense of anger or maybe guilt that *they* should have been experiencing. We look at this and emphatically state that they are wrong, yet our so called worship services are actually filled with more paganism and rituals that are no where even close to being rooted in the Word. We have traded the unfiltered gospel for motivational speaking and expect God to show up and move. Our idols have become our attachment to trying to get where somebody else or some other ministry is. We are attached to trying to prove something and to our blueprint.

While you can say amen to the fact that the state of the church needs to be addressed, let us not forget that we are a temple too. We may not be lighting incense and praying to a carved idol, but our indulgence in everything but our purpose makes us no better than these weeping for a false deity, cutting themselves, and worshipping wood. Whatever is in the way of our complete and total surrender to God, is and idol. It's an idol, and it has our time, treasure, and reverence.

Address the Apathy – The Death of Love

Where there is no awe, and no reverence, there is also no love. It is impossible to love something and demonstrate no awe or reverence for it. I cannot tell you how many times over the course of my ministry years I have encountered people who, when asked about their prayer life, coolly, casually, and even emphatically state that they just can't find the time. So let me get this straight. You want me to entreat God on your behalf, pull a whole word down from heaven, release you into your request, and you don't even care about your relationship with Him?

Now listen, I am blessed to be married. I would be hard pressed to believe that my husband actually loved me if he did everything that he could to avoid and neglect me, or only fellowshipped with me when in need of sex. Something just wouldn't sit right with me. I would be even more outraged if he said he loved me but only spoke to me through someone else. Who does that? We do. All of the time. To God.

I said earlier there is a difference between respect and reverence. Our adoration for Him should be reflected in our lifestyle of complete surrender and obedience. To limit that adoration to a series of services is ritual not love. No matter how emotional your display, you cannot actually be devoted to someone you make no time for.

God desires a love affair with us. I am not speaking in the erotic sense. When we think of delighting ourselves in Him, He wants us lost in Him—all in to Him, as we tend to be with a new love interest. He does not desire to be that rejected lover. One of the most powerful books of the Bible that demonstrates a relentless love for us is carried out through the Prophet Hosea.

Hosea was instructed to marry Gomer a prostitute, and if you actually read the book it will astound you that one could live so consistently heartbroken. We see in this book God using the marriage of Gomer and Hosea as an indictment against His people for their consistent idol worship, which He depicts as adultery. The children of Israel were named as harlots consistently lusting after every thing but God.

Even when Gomer had no intent to be faithful, Hosea is instructed to take her back in and in one case buy her back. Consistently he is riddled with trying to make Gomer behave as a wife should, but she was a harlot at heart. Without a deep and internal addressing, there would be nothing that would make her faithful.

We catch the heart of God revealed as He reminds, pleads, addresses, curses, forgives, and purposes. It's a moving tale that should bring all of us to a place of deep internal searching and complete conviction. God is relentless in His love for us, and when that love is not reciprocated from us to Him, we are the harlots, we spiritually atrophy, and Satan remains lord of our lives and maintains power and control over something we were purposed to snatch from Him.

The lack of love for God is often a lack of love for ourselves. Sometimes we are challenged to accept unconditional love because we have never known and were certainly not trained to give it. Satan does his number on us early specifically to thwart any confidence we might have in relationships. We often look at relationship with God like we do with man or woman, and we find ourselves growing easily disinterested. Further we cannot imagine what a real love affair with God can look like, so we settle for a series of services and whatever portion of His presence we get those days. The rest of the week is ours.

The subject of love is as extensive as the many reasons we fail to receive or show it. I cannot possibly address it all in one chapter, but you can take time with God to talk about where love has lacked or failed in your life and discover with

Him where there is any lack in your expression of love for Him, yourself, and others.

Paul gives us a profound discourse on love and what it should look like activated in our lives in 1 Corinthians 13, and it is more than enough to ponder.

If I could speak all the languages of earth and of angels, but didn't love others, I would only be a noisy gong or a clanging cymbal. [2] If I had the gift of prophecy, and if I understood all of God's secret plans and possessed all knowledge, and if I had such faith that I could move mountains, but didn't love others, I would be nothing. [3] If I gave everything I have to the poor and even sacrificed my body, I could boast about it; but if I didn't love others, I would have gained nothing.

Love is patient and kind. Love is not jealous or boastful or proud or rude. It does not demand its own way. It is not irritable, and it keeps no record of being wronged. [6] It does not rejoice about injustice but rejoices whenever the truth wins out. [7] Love never gives up, never loses faith, is always hopeful, and endures through every circumstance.

Prophecy and speaking in unknown languages and special knowledge will become useless. But love will last forever! [9] Now our knowledge is partial and incomplete, and even the gift of prophecy reveals only part of the whole picture! [10] But when the time of perfection comes, these partial things will become useless.

When I was a child, I spoke and thought and reasoned as a child. But when I grew up, I put away childish things. Now we see things imperfectly, like puzzling reflections in a mirror, but then we will see everything with perfect clarity. All that I know now is partial and incomplete, but then I will know everything completely, just as God now knows me completely.

Three things will last forever—faith, hope, and love—and the greatest of these is love.

Satan wants us to believe we shouldn't bother God unless we need something big, or that God is too busy to be a relational and up close and personal God. He keeps us locked in tradition because tradition is not teaching us to seek God, which is relentless pursuit of Him. He knows that relationship with God – genuine relationship, leads us out of apathy and into destiny, which means his defeat.

I wanted to address apathy more specifically in this chapter, because as we define authentic worship, we need to see clearly what we are up against in the earth and in ourselves. We needed this very brief look at just a few key ways God is often neglected and begin to address those things. Not all of us are called to the church, but all of us touch church in some way. Judgment has already begun in the house of God, and these are just a few of the things God wants addressed, but it must first begin within us.

I want to draw your attention back to our opening headlining text in this chapter.

> *I, the LORD have called you to demonstrate my righteousness. I will take you by the hand and guard you, and I will give you to My people, Israel as a symbol of my covenant with them. And you will be a light to guide the nations. You will open the eyes of the blind. You will free the captives from prison, releasing those who sit in dark dungeons. Isaiah 42:6-7*

If you have any questions about the reason for your existence, let that text sizzle in your spirit. This is the ultimate purpose for our existence, and it is how we are called to take dominion in this era. The text refers to Jesus, but has also been passed on to us as we have been commissioned to carry on His work in a variety of ways.

Pay attention to that dynamic expression. I know we are not taught to see ourselves this way, but receive it from Isaiah. We are to be a **living demonstration** of His righteousness, we are **a gift** to this generation (to His people) as **a symbol** of His covenant with us, and we are **a light** to guide **the nations**. We will open the eyes of the blind and set captives free literally and spiritually. We will get into the ways in which we are to do this, I promise, but for now take it all in. Allow yourself to imagine this kind of life that brings God such glory and draws the world's attention to Him in whatever way He chooses to do that through us.

This is huge. It is great responsibility, but with God all things are possible. All we have to do is obey and deploy. He gives us all we need. To address the state of the world today, we must first see ourselves as God sees us. We must address any apathy within ourselves, and we must trust God to take our hand, guard us, and guide us.

I want you to ponder that text and sit with it. I want you to allow God to minister to you through it. I want you to ask God for right perspective, because as we travel into the next sections, you will need to be open to seeing yourself as you never have, and you will need to be open to redefining your worship and relationship with religion.

Chapter Reflections

1. In what ways have you been apathetic in your sense of awe of God? What are some ways you can address that?

2. In what ways have you been apathetic in your sense of reverence for God? What are some ways you can address that?

3. In what ways have you been apathetic in your sense of love for God and others? What are some ways you can address that?

4. Review Isaiah 42:6-7 again. How does it shape the way you see yourself now, knowing that God is also referring to you?

Part 2

Redefining Worship: Seeing Worship as Deployment

Exploring worship with the understanding that we are a Word out of God's mouth, and a deployment in the earth to play our part in this Holy war.

CHAPTER FOUR

Jesus, Savior, Violent Blow!

> **"**
>
> **And from the days of John the Baptist until now, the kingdom of Heaven suffereth violence, and the violent take it by force.**
> **Matthew 11:12 KJV**

Up until now, we have focused on the Sovereignity of God, God's intentions for humankind, and on the deception of Satan as we have been offering the building blocks toward understanding authentic worship. In many ways we have already been defining it, but there is still so much more to discover and unpack, and we are not shy about taking the time necessary to do so, to ensure that by this book's end, you have the complete picture for why you and I exist and what that means for all of hell.

It is only befitting that we discuss Christ as His entry from eternity into time draws our attention to so much more than just His sacrifice on the cross. His entry into earth and everything that He did and how He lived are life clues for us concerning our existence, assignment, power, and authority.

Jesus – the Pre-existent God

To understand where authentic worship begins, we must first understand where Jesus began by looking at what we can only humanly articulate as the beginning of Jesus Himself. It is important to note that Jesus was not a creation of God's. That would have made Him lower than God, no; He is preexistent *with* and *as* God. He did not randomly appear in the New Testament. He is existent and highly active all throughout the Word (the Bible). It is important to discuss His "beginnings" because there have been numerous attempts to diminish and dismiss Him. Entire religions have been founded upon the rejection of Him, and on the false identifying of Him. For someone who is said to not be real, He is certainly a consistent agitator as Satan works over time to keep us from our Savior. Why so much emphasis on proving Him irrelevant and unreal or diminished to a prophet and teacher? Again, we see here Satan's hand in keeping us from our Savior by confusing us with so many religions, false Gods, and critiques of God Himself and His written word. We see him at work as we look at what evangelicalism has been founded upon and how even in its subtleties it is reproducing a demonic agenda to suppress important truth about who God's people are. O yes! Satan is a cunning one. His fear of Jesus, and His attempts to dissuade us from Him are essentially because he too knew Jesus as preexistent—as God—and his every endeavor is a battle for the worship and exalting of himself above God. Through understanding the preexistence of Jesus, we gain clear insight as to the reason the adversary is so desperate in His attempts to sequester information about who He is, and therefore who we are to become.

The Bible says that Jesus always existed. God is multiplicitous and manifold meaning He is many expressions of Himself that would be impossible to articulate except by His revelation. Even then we could spend a lifetime trying to learn Him. We just note that everything He created does not exist apart from Him; therefore He is many and all. The concept of God pulling Himself out of Himself is not new. We see it at the creation of Adam when He says; "*Come let us make man in our image.*" Pulling Himself out of Himself in the expression of Jesus the Son should not surprise us then. Psychologically we want to separate them, but they are one.

Most critical to our faith—or most pertinent is our Trinitarian belief, which can be proven in the Word. The trinity is God as Father, Son, and Holy Spirit. John 3:16 refers to God the Father's relationship with His Son, but does not suggest Jesus was a created being. Jesus is God and during eternity past coexisted with God the Father in Heaven. How God chooses to articulate and manifest Himself in any form is not up for critique from me. I accept Jesus as both part of Him as Son and as Him, God. Still, we can look to the Word for further proof.

Prior to His earthly ministry, Jesus along with God the Father (1 Corinthians 8:6), the Holy Spirit (Genesis 1:1-2, Job 33:4), created the world we live in (Hebrews 1:1-2, Colossians 1:16, Ephesians 3:9). **STOP** and read those texts.

John 1:1 tells us that *in the beginning was the Word, and the Word was with God, and the Word was God.* The expression of the Word also serves as another name for Jesus. We see it in Revelations 19:13, 1 John 1:1-4, and John 1:14-15. Particular emphasis on John 1:3 refers to Jesus as the Word and tells us all things were made by Him (Jesus) and without Him or apart from Him, nothing was made that was made.

Long before Jesus was a swaddling infant in the arms of His earthly parents or a "rebellious" adolescent journeying to teach in the temple without notifying them, He existed, and He visited earth on more than one occasion. Genesis 81:1 speaks of the LORD appearing to Abraham. God appeared to Abraham as three men, two angels and Jesus. Genesis 32:24-32 records a visit in which God (Jesus) wrestled with Jacob. In Joshua the 5th chapter verses 13-15, God (Jesus) visits and encourages Joshua for battle most likely in the likeness of an angel or a man that would have stood out as a heavenly being. Again, how God chose to represent Himself in any of these cases was solely up to Him and remains His understanding.

Lastly, Jesus also testifies to His own preexistence (John 17: 5, 24). In John 3:13 He says, *no one has ever gone into heaven except the one that came from heaven—the Son of man* (Jesus Christ). On another occasion, Jesus was teaching in the temple after the Feast of Tabernacles and says, *"I am the light of the world* (John 8:12). He further explains His origins as of His Father in Heaven.

Satan knew exactly whom he was up against. Prior to expulsion he had seen Him, became a guardian for Him, knew Him and admired Him and wanted to *be* Him. Here in the earth is the greatest plot twist hell would ever know – God Himself come down in the person of Jesus for an epic battle!

Jesus – the Revolutionary Blow: Eternity Invading Time.

Prior to the arrival of Jesus as God in the earth, a trip through the Old Testament reveals previous patterns. If you've ever done an in depth study of Exodus, Leviticus, and Numbers, you might have found yourself moving from glorious adventure to being drawn into complete boredom by all the laws and regulations, sacrifices and sin offerings. God had established under the old law a system for atonement. His reckless and easily enticed chosen people were consistent in their rebellion, which made God consistent in His punishments. In His Sovereignity and mercy, He would call forth a prophet or a judge to remind the people to turn back and live.

Satan was well aware that this time would come as God addressed him prophetically during the fall of man (Genesis 3:14). What we also know; is that the birth of Jesus incarnate was such a violent blow to the kingdom of hell that attempts were put out on His life before He exited the womb. Firstborn sons were slaughtered en masse in the hopes of eliminating any possible messiah.

When Satan disrupted God's intentions for humanity, shots were fired. He initiated an entire holy war, and what we see by the entry of God incarnate (Jesus) is an escalation of divine authority and power come to put Satan in his place once and for all, and Satan was *not* ready. Not as much as he thought he was.

Paul describes Jesus' earth invasion by quoting from the psalm (Psalm 40:6-8) in Hebrews 10:8-9

> *Sacrifices and offerings and burnt offerings and sacrifices for sin You did not desire nor delight in (which were offered according to the law), He then has said, "Behold, I have come to do your will. "He takes away the first that He may establish the second.*

What is "the first" and what is "the second?" The first here refers to the first covenant, the old covenant with all its sacrifices; the second refers to the second covenant, the new covenant with Christ as the unique sacrifice, a part of God incarnate come to redeem the world Himself and prove to the rest of humanity something extraordinary in them by the example of Jesus as man and God.

Man was doomed to die in his sins as no ritual sacrifice was serving as complete and total atonement. God, who made a promise that man would reign with Him eternally again –and I am using very intentional language when I say this, commissioned His own self into incarnation to come and put away animal sacrifices and establish Himself – His own body as the unique sacrifice to terminate God's old economy and establish a new one. We have seen before the termination of an old economy when God destroyed life with a flood. God promised after which to never do again, and becomes His own strategy for complete redemption. Plot twist!

We emphasize Christ as God here because as is typical in religion we emphasize the Father, Son, and Holy Spirit, as 3 individual units although we readily recite they are one. We don't consistently mentally perceive that Jesus *is* God because we talk about Him so much individually, but He was nonetheless God incarnate and we must not forget that as it also speaks to God in us, which we will get to.

The emphasis here is new covenant that cannot be stopped because who sacrificed a part of Himself is not flawed. He is the only true redemption. Calling that part of Himself "Son" is of no consequence. Whatever He called His relationship, Jesus is no less He. God is consistent in His revelatory announcements about relationships be it naming His people as prostitutes or expressing Christ as His son. What's most important is understanding the sentiment and the magnitude of His sacrifices for us in a way that we can feel and appreciate.

I know what it is to be a scorned love, rejected lover, to be cheated on and disrespected, overlooked, and devalued. I am a mother who has not known the pain of the loss of a child, but I have loved and still love my children deeply enough to sense the possible agony of losing any one or all of them with deep sorrow for it without experiencing it. I have lost a brother who was murdered and could sense very deeply the internal agony of my own mother. God in His mercy and relentless love and pursuit of us gave of Himself to establish a new covenant that could not be cancelled by man's errors and choices. The enemy wanted to pack out his kingdom with the generations of men, but He is completely defeated by a magnanimous offering that we can never really repay.

Understanding and emphasizing Jesus as God removes supposed contradiction of child sacrifice. Irresponsible men have considered the crucifixion detestable, but the wiser understand it as inevitable and yes, sacrificial, but in the right context.

I have stated that Satan initiated this Holy War. Only God understood what it would take for man to be fully redeemed. Satan may not be as powerful as God, but he is a master manipulator and excels at influencing the enticements and actions of men. God being all knowing understood the evil hearts of men and their lusts and the revolution His invasion in the earth would be. He understood before ever there was an age of man the gross negligence of pure worship, which would be traded for religious lust for power. Jesus' entry and His message would be a radical one that would expose evil for what it was on all fronts, and He would be demonically "set up" for it.

It was always known to God the true hearts of men and their enticements, their wicked deception and preservation of it at all costs. There were laws that if twisted just enough could create the "need" for an unfair and unnecessary and unjust humiliating death. God knowing all this chose to release Himself as Jesus in the earth with His only concern as Himself as a worthy sacrifice. Knowing He would be rejected, He still incarnated and accepted the inevitable. God is not some sadistic God who condemns child sacrifice then turns and does the same. That is simply not so. The world was then and remains cruel and satanic, and murder was inevitable for a radicalist like Jesus to be claiming to be God, performing miracles and threatening the establishment. It was inevitable, not *ideal*—the gross consequence of a holy war—and God still said, "I'll go." "I'll send a part of Myself to take care of this once and for all."

I believe that when we make statements we should be able to back them up in scripture. I have submitted for your consideration that Jesus is God as they are one. I have expressed that God is not a sadist and that crucifixion was inevitable and we shouldn't perceive it as a sadistic act, but one that was meant to be in the midst of a holy war.

Jesus (God incarnate) explains it this way:

From the days of John the Baptist until now, the kingdom of Heaven suffereth violence, and the violent take it by force. Matthew 11:12 KJV

At the time Jesus has spoken this, John is in jail about to be beheaded. He has sent messengers to Jesus to ask if He is truly the Messiah or if he should look for another. Jesus in His discourse reminds the messengers of all He has done, in essence drawing their attention that His works have demonstrated God in the earth, and then he shares that the kingdom of heaven has been consistently under violent attack. People have tried to force their way into God's kingdom (namely Satan and then it is seen in his influence over kings and religious leaders).

I said earlier that shots were fired when Satan's deception interrupted God's intentions. We saw it again in the days of Noah. Here in the days of Jesus, Him as eternity invading earth, bringing the Kingdom down to earth was also a violent interruption to the kingdom of hell. Walking in truth and against the world's system would come with a price.

As Jesus is giving His discourse about John, in it He is drawing our attention to the warfare and the humility of it all. Only those that humble themselves in the sight of God would inherit the kingdom. He did not come as a majestic king, but instead a humble servant to sacrifice Himself for the good and redemption of all mankind. The people would want a radical revolutionary with a great army, all of which could have been summoned, but instead they would get a King that would submit to being a slaughtered lamb, for redemption they could never have imagined. John the Baptist was a type of sacrificial lamb and in Jesus' celebration of Him and the truths He speaks in that text, He is exposing the inevitably of death even for Himself because violent men, wicked men, could not accept or embrace a humble or repentant lifestyle. They would continue in their wickedness but yet expect to reign with God in the end, and it was simply asinine to believe such things. They were absolutely deceived and relentless in their attempt to maintain their illusions.

A crucifixion would seem like a total loss, but a resurrection would change life, faith, and kingdom forever!

Jesus Transfigured & Why it Matters

I said this earlier; Jesus did not come to start a religion! In fact, being a believer in Jesus is not a religion at all. Perhaps we must then define religion so that you'll understand the point. Every religion is a particular system of faith and worship. It is manmade and actually misses the entire point of Christ as it often presently plays out. Religion is mankind's attempt to package faith and a deity, to establish a set of guidelines and rules for living and worshipping, and then promote it to be replicated and carried out. When we think of religion we tend to see it as a set of guidelines to abide by in order to please a deity. There is some good to the fellowship, don't misunderstand, but to actually *be* Christian is to be an imitator of Christ. There is no part of that that can be packaged or established by a set of rules and regulations. Christ is to be worshipped yes, but worshipped through lifestyle not soulish and emotional activity or good works.

We have talked at length about creation and being formed with the same nature, but seeing ourselves that way often poses a challenge. We cannot be imitators of Jesus except we have His nature, and we must accept the fact that we do. I spoke earlier about the inevitability of becoming like my mother and my children becoming like me. What we are around consistently has its influence on us. When the early church was established at Antioch they were called Christians, not just because they followed Christ, but also because they reminded the people of Christ. They carried His spiritual DNA and looked like Him and behaved like Him. We are supposed to be that same expression. When people see us, we should be a reminder to them—physical evidence that God is real! Being a follower of Christ, a Christian, or a believer, however you choose to name yourself is not a matter of rituals but *identity* and *relationship.*

We are not commanded to live *for* God. God is to be made visible to the earth alive *in* us. We are called to live *with* Him. It's a living breathing relationship that changes every aspect of our lives. We take on His nature and then express that nature in the earth. The same power He wielded, the same authority He carried, and the same connection with God the Father is *in* us. Jesus is not a task list or a list of rules and behaviors to abide by. He is God incarnate and died to bring us back into the intended relationship with God. We are the temples God Himself dwells in. If only we could really grasp that and take that to heart. What a difference it would make in how we live, move, and speak!

Religion places too much emphasis on our own ability, and we soon find ourselves frustrated, depressed, and disillusioned, and in a constant state of flux because we are trying to earn something freely given by way of the cross. It is not that we shouldn't be concerned with holy living, of course we should be. We should not continue in sin that grace may abound, God forbid, but trying to live by a set of rules does not give us the experience God desires for us. It binds us to monitoring works. If God's abode is inside us, and He is the one with all power, if we are created in His image, and if we are formed by His hands, then when we yield ourselves to Him completely, He can be the fullness of expression of Himself through us as He wants to be. The world does not need another religion. There are plenty of those. The world needs to see a true and living God so active in us, so demonstrated through us and in us, that they will be completely drawn to Him.

Religion is a blocker. Within its confines we are always trying to "make it in" instead of pulling kingdom down to invade earth. We are often told that we are poor wretched souls doomed to die if we don't get it right, but does that sound like beings created in God's image? I mean, yes, without Him we are doomed to eternal damnation, but how we see ourselves as His agents matters. If we are always lowly wretched souls who should be watching our every step for fear of tripping into hell, who is going to demonstrate God and the power and thriving and good that He is? God is not wretched, He is all-powerful, amazingly creative, extraordinarily good, and He Himself has declared His own works good! You are His work, you are good, and you carry *His* DNA. When you became a kingdom citizen through Christ, you were justified and no longer wretched but victorious.

We shouldn't be looking for credits for good behavior. We should be making the world hunger to know Him whenever we step into the atmosphere just like Jesus did. I know you weren't trained to see yourself as a type of Jesus or as put here on a similar Jesus mission. We can never measure up or compare. I feel you on that, but He spoke greater works in you. Don't let religion and the need to bend to *the system* strangulate your purpose or keep God from being made active in you. It only leads to a defeated life no one around you will ever be motivated to want.

We must stop presenting God as a poor and lowly creature, powerless and inactive who has no control. All of who He is can flow from us as we let Him in and in turn pour Him back out into the earth. If we wonder why we struggle to draw anybody into kingdom, it's our presentation. In trying to live into a packaged and marketed campaign, we become angry, frustrated, bitter, mean, nasty, agitated, self-righteous, you name it. Who wants that? We get enough of that in the world.

Jesus did not come to make us religious. He came to make us alive and full of His wonders.

There's a moment in Christ's history I would like to draw your attention to, it is Jesus' moment of transfiguration as recorded in Matthew 17.

> *Six days later Jesus took Peter and the two brothers, James and John, and led them up a high mountain to be alone. As the men watched, Jesus' appearance was transformed so that his face shone like the sun, and his clothes became as white as light. [3] Suddenly, Moses and Elijah appeared and began talking with Jesus.*
>
> *Peter exclaimed, "Lord, it's wonderful for us to be here! If you want, I'll make three shelters as memorials—one for you, one for Moses, and one for Elijah."*
>
> *But even as he spoke, a bright cloud overshadowed them, and a voice from the cloud said, "This is my dearly loved Son, who brings me great joy. Listen to him." [6] The disciples were terrified and fell face down on the ground.*
>
> *Then Jesus came over and touched them. "Get up," he said. "Don't be afraid." And when they looked up, Moses and Elijah were gone, and they saw only Jesus.*

And verses 14-20

At the foot of the mountain, a large crowd was waiting for them. A man came and knelt before Jesus and said, "Lord, have mercy on my son. He has seizures and suffers terribly. He often falls into the fire or into the water. So I brought him to your disciples, but they couldn't heal him."

Jesus said, "You faithless and corrupt people! How long must I be with you? How long must I put up with you? Bring the boy here to me." [18] *Then Jesus rebuked the demon in the boy, and it left him. From that moment the boy was well.*

Afterward the disciples asked Jesus privately, "Why couldn't we cast out that demon?"

"You don't have enough faith," Jesus told them. "I tell you the truth, if you had faith even as small as a mustard seed, you could say to this mountain, 'Move from here to there,' and it would move. Nothing would be impossible."

These texts reveal so much about destiny, but it begins with transformation, and if you follow our ministry, then you know transformation and deployment are my favorite subjects.

We tend to read this passage and kind of glaze over it to focus on certain parts of it, but I am not sure that we fully grasp what happened here—or to be more specific, what it is communicating to us about worship and the lasting impact it leaves on our lives.

I want to draw your attention first to the fact that they travelled upward. We are used to language that suggests elevation comes with descension and that usually relates to humility and kneeling in prayer. That's good. It has its truth. Here though I would like to challenge that concept and suggest that elevations begin with ascension. The kind of elevation I am referring to, is not how many fliers you can see your face on, how full your calendar will become, or how many television appearances you will make. All that is good, but what good is any of that if you have no God to carry with you?

To ascend is to leave your current position and move up higher. What we need most from God is not on the level we are standing on. Whatever is next for us, we must climb up into Him to receive. We must ascend to where He is.

There is a powerful revelation in Genesis 28:10-16. Jacob is resting when he has this vision we all hear commonly referred to as Jacob's ladder. In this vision Jacob is watching angels ascend and descend, in that order. Ascension was first. As he is watching this unfold, he hears the voice of God promise him that he will in fact inherit the land promised to his fathers.

Inheritance required ascension up into the presence of God, and from that time with God comes a descension to carry down what God has released into the earth. Those angels were commissioned to climb up into the presence of God through intercession and then release the promise and power of God into the earth. This is *"Thy will be done on earth as it is in Heaven."* Remember earlier we talked about Satan having robbed Adam of living in the presence of God and how if He had been allowed to, the results would have been an earth blanketed in people born into the presence and therefore being the presence? This has that same significance.

God made a promise, and the text is a demonstration of how we collect that promise (spiritual ascension), and then release it into the earth (descension). Our lives should be a series of ascensions and decensions.

Back to Jesus and the apostles, we find that as Jesus ascended to the place where God was, he literally transforms! This wrecks me in a good way every time. Jesus has the revelation already on who He is, and so here we find that this ascension is the *continued* work of climbing high up into God in order to consistently flow with His will. Jesus maintained a lifestyle of living in the Presence of God, and He was therefore able to execute the will of the Father at any given moment. At this particular time, Peter, James, and John were given the phenomenal opportunity to witness ascension and what it produces.

The Bible tells us that while they stood on the mountain, Jesus literally transformed into a light as bright as the sun and began to converse with Moses and Elijah. How astoundingly powerful it must have been to witness that. Right before their eyes, they witness an ascension that leads to a visible transformation. This is what ascension does; it transforms us from one state of being to the next. It releases something into us to be expressed out of us into the earth.

Peter being amazed wanted to stop and build three altars. I feel you Peter. It was a powerful moment that he wanted to remember forever, but he almost missed the revelation of it. He did what religion does. He parked in an emotional experience and most likely wanted to be able to come back to that place and relive it. God; however, is multiplicitous revelation. No one encounter we have with Him is meant to be a one and done or worshipped forever. That encounter was for *that* moment for what needed to be carried into the earth at that exact time.

I remember when I got my first car. I was so excited. I had saved all my paychecks and I was finally able to go to the BMW car lot with some old friends and purchase the vehicle I had seen advertised. When I got there and sat in the car to be my own. I felt even more excitement at the thought of being the possible owner. Everything worked out, and I was able to purchase the car. It would have made no sense if after I went through all that to obtain my dream vehicle, I paid, said my thank you, and then left the car on the lot parked. It was mine to drive, to take home. I worked hard for it. I now owned it, and the next thing to do was to drive it off the lot and put it to use.

In religion we settle for parking at a lot of emotional experiences. God does all He can to reveal Himself to us at many a revival and conference, and after all His magnificent display, we don't carry Him anywhere. We leave Him there to meet us next gathering, and neither we nor anyone else that could have benefited from an impartation from what we were meant to carry out of these experiences receives much of anything. We adhere to the program and when the program is done so are we.

It was not time for Peter to build an altar there. That's not worship. Worship is taking what you ascended to receive back down into the earth so everyone else can experience it. We see the truth of that statement in the next thing that happens. Just before they leave the ascension, God speaks audibly to affirm whom Jesus is and to *implore* them to listen to Him.

As they get to the bottom of the hill, a father approaches Jesus because his child is possessed. He had asked the disciples to help, but they had no power to cast it out. Jesus offers a stern rebuke because they had been with Him. They had seen Him do so much, but they had no faith that they too could do the same. They were still unsure of Jesus' identity and without that revelation and clarity, they could not flow in their own, which would have been expressed if they had faith and relationship.

We know the word. We know we can do greater works but we lack the faith and understanding that we are a resource in order to perform.

I too made this mistake, and I made it in front of my children, which I hate. I have moved passed it, but I often revisit the moment when it comes to these conversations.

I had just finished preaching and I had to stop by the bank to make a deposit. Where that particular bank was, there was a thrift store. My daughter and I love a good thrift store and a Dollar Tree. It's our thing. I am crafty, so I am always finding something I can repurpose or build.

As we were exiting the store, there was a lady walking toward us just about to enter the thrift store. We stepped aside to let her through and proceeded to walk to the car. My son must have looked back because he alerted me she wanted our attention. We turned around and walked toward her, and her hand gestures signaled to us that she was deaf. I know a little sign language, but I didn't have to use it. She said a few things I could barely make out but suddenly, as if God decided to speak for her, she started talking clearly.

She said she could tell that we were churchgoers and asked me to pray with her. It was so clear I never would have assumed she had ever been deaf. What assured me she was, was that after that, her words were no longer clear. She spoke again as if she had never been able to hear and relied on hand gestures and grunts to communicate. We all held hands and I began to pray. I didn't look down or away because she was deaf, but to my surprise, she was head bowed and saying yes lord and amen to all my words. I prayed for all that I could think of, and when I was done, she lifted her head and said a clear thank you and went back to gestures and grunts. I promise you it was a miracle. She managed to eek out that she could actually hear every word and had been deaf since childhood.

My kids and I were floored. We walked away with such zeal and excitement and praise for God. We came home and shared it with my husband. Every time I am in that city I think of that amazing exchange.

Here is what I missed. I parked. I did what Peter did. I praised for the experience and let the experience have too much of my time. Because I didn't sense my identity (right after preaching mind you), I missed an opportunity to restore her hearing completely. God showed me it was possible. All I had to do was agree and pull Him down into the moment. I prayed for everything concerning her but her full restoration. It was not the will of God for her to be deaf. When confronted with an opportunity to demonstrate God to her and in front of everyone standing on, I missed it. I completely missed it. It never even crossed my mind, and that bothers me to this day. There is no following God without being always tapped into Him. There is no genuine following of God without expectancy. Without expectancy, we leave others to their fate and may even pray for them amiss as I did that day. When we carry the presence of God, no one should leave our presence the same. I wasn't walking in the fullness of my identity and that woman remained deaf. The apostles were not walking in the fullness of their identity or a real revelation of Christ just yet, and because of that, the boy could not be released from demonic possession and torment.

We cannot settle for emotional encounters. We should be ascending to fill up on God and receive transformation and then descending with it to release it into the earth. Our worship (to be more defined later) is our ascension. The more we worship, the more God can release more of Himself into us, and that is the more we can be forever authorized to give out. It's not just for special people. There are some people that God highlights only as a witness to their availability to Him and the possibilities, but miracles, signs, and wonders are supposed to follow all believers. That is a promise. If more of us did it, the church and the earth would be in awe of God. I believe at this time in history there is a great awakening happening and we will again see these great moves of God, because more people are discovering there is much more to faith, and they are willing to step into something higher in order to release more of God in the earth. Don't' let any transfiguration/transformation moment pass you by. It's not a one and done. It's consistent ascension and descension.

Restoration of Kingdom Keys

We talked earlier about Satan having taken the keys to the kingdom, our dominion and eternal life, and having robbed us of growing up in the presence of God and perceiving ourselves as in the image of God. This holy war that we were born into is all about exercising the power and authority post Christ's ascension, and essentially snatching those keys back from the hands of the enemy. The journey of Jesus is an example of that as well. First, what are the keys to the kingdom?

> *When Jesus came to the region of Caesarea Philippi, he asked his disciples, "Who do people say the Son of Man is?" They replied, "Some say John the Baptist; others say Elijah; and still others, Jeremiah or one of the prophets." "But what about you?" he asked. "Who do you say I am?" Simon Peter answered, "You are the Messiah, the Son of the living God." Jesus replied, "Blessed are you, Simon son of Jonah, for this was not revealed to you by flesh and blood, but by my Father in heaven. And I tell you that you are Peter, and on this rock I will build my church, and the gates of Hades will not overcome it. I will give you the **keys of the kingdom** of heaven; whatever you bind on earth will be bound in heaven, and whatever you loose on earth will be loosed in heaven." Then he ordered his disciples not to tell anyone that he was the Messiah.* Matthew 16: 13-20

Christianity.com explains this concept excellently in their article "What are the Keys of the Kingdom?"

> *In both the Old and New Testaments, keys symbolize power and authority. The nature of that power and authority varies depending on the context. Isaiah 22:22 refers to "the key of the house of David," which in the context refers to the authority of the steward who manages*

the household of the king. That same imagery is applied to the risen Christ (Revelations 3:7), who also has "the keys of Death and Hades" (Revelations 1:18). In Luke 11:52, Jesus claims that the experts in the Jewish Law "have taken away the key of knowledge." In other words, through their hypocrisy they have not only failed to enter the kingdom of God themselves, but have prevented others from entering as well.

This reference to the key of knowledge sheds light on the expression "keys of the kingdom" here. Through Peter's faithful proclamation of the gospel, Peter will open the door of the kingdom to those who respond in faith, while at the same time keeping it shut from those who do not. Because the gospel determines what is bound and what is loosed, Peter's actions of binding and loosing here on earth express heaven's verdict itself.

The keys to the kingdom are the authority that we have through Jesus alive in us to render a verdict on any situation, and call it back into alignment with the perfect and intended will of God. Read that again.

Before we can have access to this authority, we must first have a revelation on who Jesus is/ who God is. That's in part what this book attempts to establish. Jesus is not a religion. He is God... *alive.* Understanding then that Jesus is meant to be active in us, and our imitation of Him means doing all He did and greater (as He stated), we must seek until we see Him alive and functioning in us. The ascension we talked about earlier that is essentially being transformed in His presence is necessary. We cannot get a revelation of Him and then fail or refuse to be transformed to carry it. God wants all authority in every area down here back into the hands of the ones He willed it to.

Imagine being left with an inheritance, and having an impostor parade as you living off the benefits that were intended for you. We would not casually dismiss it. We would provide proof of identity and do all we could to expose and take from the impostor what rightfully belongs to us. It should be the same with our attitude toward Satan. Why let him parade around the earth with keys that should be in our hands that can be used to unlock more of God in the earth? If we are truly believers, this should be our highest priority and foremost concern. Everything we do should have the intended consequence of expanding and building the kingdom and expelling what is not God's intended will. We cannot lead people to a God we are not interested in knowing, and we cannot wield power and authority from a false identity.

Authority & Power over Death

In earlier chapters we learned that Satan's deception and man's fall initiated a time limit on human life. Jesus' violent entry into the earth against Satan, and His death and resurrection snatched death out of the hands of Satan and restored our right to eternal life. On several occasions we witness the miracle working power of Jesus through His raising of the dead. I want to draw your attention here to a story most of us are familiar with found in John 11:11-15 regarding Lazarus.

> Then he said, "Our friend Lazarus has fallen asleep, but now I will go and wake him up."
>
> The disciples said, "Lord, if he is sleeping, he will soon get better!" They thought Jesus meant Lazarus was simply sleeping, but Jesus meant Lazarus had died.
>
> So he told them plainly, "Lazarus is dead. And for your sakes, I'm glad I wasn't there, for now you will really believe. Come, let's go see him."

Lazarus was not a stranger to Jesus. He was a relative of Martha's and was probably quite close to Jesus. Jesus even names Lazarus in the text as a friend. So why not go immediately when He received the news? Something else was more important. Whatever it was God wanted to do with that moment was a priority over any emotional response anyone was having.

Sometimes as we stand with God, we will find ourselves in opposition with those we love. I remember being expected to be in attendance at an event because of my relationship with someone, But God made it so clear to me that He was not in that, and was not giving me clearance to go. I knew that my absence would speak volumes and I would surely hear the chatter about it and face the wrath of it later, but God communicated to me that if I thought my absence was going to look bad for not attending, I should consider that my presence would also communicate volumes, and I would be perceived as affirming what He opposed just by showing up. Sometimes we lose sight of who we are and we don't appreciate the weight of what we carry. God was intentional in developing a certain reputation with me whether I wanted it or not, and He reminded me that everything I do is done from the place of my true identity. There can be no compromise in that. My absence cost me that relationship, but I would rather not be at odds with God. When God is trying to communicate something in a moment, many will not understand it because we don't always see the spiritual implications, and the instructions weren't given to them. Like Jesus, we must stand on the side of God at all costs, even when it hurts. There are some things we have to stay out of or away from, and it will make sense down the road. I digress.

Jesus delayed visiting Lazarus when he was sick, knowing that Lazarus would die. Though He could have healed Lazarus (even from a distance), He told His disciples that He was glad He was not there. Jesus anticipated the Resurrection that He would perform as a sign to His disciples, that they might believe. The greater good here is that disciples needed to experience Jesus' authority over death in an up close and personal way. It would be so necessary for their understanding and their faith for the journey ahead – that being both Jesus' crucifixion and their continued journey in the earth without Him.

Jesus arrives, and after a brief conversation with Martha rebuking her for her lack of faith, we read that Jesus weeps. Lets put a pin in that.

Although John does not tell us specifically why Jesus wept, we can infer one reason from the context: Jesus was grieved over death as the result of mankind's sin.

The Apostle Paul confirmed the correlation between sin and death: *"Therefore, just as through one man sin entered the world, and death through sin, and thus death spread to all men, because all sinned"* (Romans 5:12). Paul also clearly wrote that *"the wages of sin is death"* in Romans 6:23.

Death is an **enemy**! We have been taught to receive it as a normal inevitability, but death was not God's intention. In raising Lazarus, Jesus showed a small glimpse of His ultimate authority over death, and thereafter He went to the cross to defeat death permanently. Death has been defeated (2 Timothy 1:10) and one day it will be destroyed forever (Revelation 20:14). Jesus refused to accept the finality of death, and neither should we. What do you mean Prophet?

Jesus had the authority to raise the dead, and by us having Jesus alive in us, we have the power to reject death as well. Does that mean that we can reverse death completely? No. Death is a permanent reality. But there are times, if we believe and carry God alive in us the way that we are meant to, we can rebuke death and push it back into hell from whence it came. We hear stories often of how a couple's baby died but through worship and prayer the baby lived. People have testified honestly that they died on operation tables or in their homes etc., and by intercession and worship (obedience); they were raised to life again.

Jesus has not changed. God's authority has not relented. God's power is not powerless to perform. He is the same God yesterday, today, and forever more. We should not assume that we do not have the power to raise the dead just as Jesus and other apostles did. We have heard of it in our time, and we should believe that the same authority is in us as we have Him. It may seem scary to think that we can step out on that kind of faith and see the miraculous happen, but as we ascend up into Him as we discussed earlier, He can coach and release us into that kind of power. Miracles, signs and wonders are supposed to follow us.

Does this mean that we should raid funerals and intercede over caskets or show up at morgues and command cadavers to live? Not unless you have a real unction from God. That would be quite a miracle indeed to grave rob and raise all the dead in a cemetery. Whew. My point here is that we are not to neglect any part of who He is. A rejection of any part of Him is to lie on Him by rendering Him incapable through us. If you believe that any part of Him is incapable, why serve? Why believe at all? He doesn't want your respect of Him as a distant God who did things in the past. He wants a relationship so infused with Him in you that He can work through you to accomplish the impossible in the *now*.

Jesus had the strategy for when to move and when to stand still. He said in John 5:30, "*I can do nothing on my own. I judge as God tells me. Therefore, my judgment is just, because I carry out the will of the one who sent me, not my own will.*" I will say this again here, and again later. Jesus *lived* in the presence of God. He was God yes, but took on human form and lived as **human** to model the possibilities. He did nothing apart from the Father, which meant He had a constant understanding of God's will in any given moment and was able to execute according to it. You and I can exercise that same authority, but it requires that we live in His presence and develop a keen sense of Him at all times.

Two pseudo aunts of mine passed away of cancer. Both had had quite a long battle with chemotherapy over the years, and both got to a place where they refused to continue the treatments. They made peace with the disease and accepted death as the next best alternative. I remember getting the news and being deeply saddened and angry. Don't misunderstand. I have no judgment for them in my heart. I was not the one living with cancer, and I certainly didn't have to face firsthand their daily struggles. All I could be was a bystander watching them face this hurdle and accept that they were just plain tired of it.

My point here is that I had a revelation that they didn't have. That fact angered me. These were women who served God faithfully my entire life. It seemed so unfair for them to be going through this, but what was staggering to me more so was that there remained such an absence of teaching believers their true identity. As I sought God about it, He reminded me that they exercised their will for their reasons. He does not override us, but He was grieved with me that they had never been taught or experienced anything other than whatever religion dished out. They served faithfully through works, but they never received the advanced course in what it means to carry God within us. They understood prayer, but they were starved in the knowledge of their true Identity. That's when God made clear to me the necessity of transformation and self-discovery through His eyes and not my own. What we agree with, we live out. What we accept we receive. He said to me that it was not His desire for them to die. They accepted a fate that they didn't have to. That bothered me.

I said that to say, I understand why Jesus wept. As much as the people saw Him do, including raising the dead, many of them still would not believe. By rejecting truth and relationship, they were accepting a fate of death that God did not intend or want for them. By missing His message to identify themselves through Him with Kingdom perspective, they were sealing their own doom. That did not surprise Jesus, but it did grieve Him.

The point I wish to emphasize here on the subject of authority over death is to not minimize or reject any part of Him and who He can be in you, whether it is to literally raise the dead or to expose someone to kingdom life to spare them eternal damnation. Yes, we have read the end of the story. We understand what is to come, but that should make us more driven to release God into the earth as much as possible. We should care. The fact that many of us have become fatalists, leaving people to their own demise, is not a reflection of being sanctified and set apart. It is arrogant and uncaring, cowardly and inappropriate. We have a job to do. There will be many who will not listen, but there will be many who will. If we all do the work of ascension into Him, we can always sense Him and defeat every demonic strategy including death.

Our Commission Post Jesus' Ascension

So what does God want us do in the earth now? We have learned so much thus far, but what is our role now? Earlier we talked about Apathy and addressing our areas of it, that is absolutely the start. We looked at Jesus' life as a model and hit on some key things that are also necessary for fulfilling what God intended. We told you that you needed to carry God into the earth, and in the next chapter we will certainly explain that further.

One of the greatest revivals man has known is recorded in the book of Acts. When they were all in the upper room (there's that ascension notion again), availing themselves to the Presence of God, the Word says that they had a mighty encounter with the Holy Spirit and an entire region was drawn into the presence of God that day. How amazing is that? Peter then preached and converted some thousands of souls. Now that's revival. Notice though that all they did was wait before God?

When we talk about what we should be doing Post Jesus, sometimes we make that conversation more complicated than necessary. A popular preacher in my area stated that people often ask him to pray for them to live their purpose. He emphatically states that he knows what their purpose is—heal the sick, raise the dead, do as Jesus did. I too have told you that we should essentially mimic Him. I do not take that back. But I want to be clearer here. We should not get caught up in any few aspects of what He did outwardly. Those are just a few things. He said that we would do greater works, and greater works simply means more. In both the Hebrew and Greek translations, greater does mean grand, big, and sizeable, but it also means important, significant, impactful, and momentous. Sometimes we perceive things as greater than others, but I want to challenge that thought. *Everything* God tells us to do is necessary and salvific. Therefore no instruction we receive from Him is minor.

I am glad that we have the authority to raise the dead and heal the sick, and open blinded eyes. Those things are profound. We should not limit the possibilities. God wants us to know Him so well that we do not reject any part of Him or His ability to demonstrate these parts of Him through us, but that conversation that God tells you to have with the woman who looks forlorn at the bus stop is equally as momentous and impactful to the Kingdom as any of the above miracles we lifted. We will explore this next chapter, but that song He tells you to write, that business He tells you to open, that non-profit He says start, that book He tells you to write, communion He tells you to take to the sick and shut in, are all equally as grand and momentous simply because whatever comes out of His mind to your ears and heart is magnificent because He is.

I have been blessed to travel the world doing ministry, and I have seen firsthand the obsession and fascination with casting out demons and performing certain miracles. We must be very careful not to glorify gifts above the gift giver. Me preaching a sermon that shifts the people's perspective and you actually raising someone from the dead does not make me any less than you or your demonstration of God in that way any better than mine.

I remember being in a service where God used me greatly to prophesy and set so many people free. Afterward, the first lady said to me that I was going to get so sharp in the prophetic that God would use me to call out credit card numbers, names and addresses. The people began to applaud, but I was immediately vexed. I could sense that God was not pleased, and I made it a point to talk to Him about it later.

In her mind, that was the ultimate experience of becoming a premier prophet, and in her ignorance, she had completely disregarded all that God had done in that moment. She dismissed it (most likely unintentionally). We went for hours that day. People went home and brought people back to the service. They practically held me hostage, but I was not to move until God was through. He healed the sick, He cast out demons, He launched ministries and businesses, I mean there was no stone left unturned minus some of the miracles Jesus did. In her mind, after all that, I would be considered "greater" if I could just add calling out credit card numbers to the mix?

I remember God saying to me that she was foolish. He was not pleased that after such a powerful demonstration of Him, she still perceived something completely irrelevant was missing. He asked me what point calling out credit card numbers would make, and He explained that if He chooses to do so, it is for His purposes, but my only aspiration should be to hear from Him and say and do what He tells me. Her assumption that calling out names, addresses, and card numbers would prove me as even more authentic was misguided. He told me that He might one day use me to do so if He chooses, but we don't strive for anything but complete obedience, and we are not to covet any aspect of what God does through anyone. I was accurate because I obeyed God. In Him there is no error. There was no need for me to "be sharper" than complete obedience.

There is no such thing as a "master prophet" simply because they have more years invested in it. We serve the same God, and God does not minor and majorly speak to us in that sense. He does not decide that because someone has an extra year over me in the work that He will use them any greater. Time may afford you more experiences in the field, but not necessarily more authority. We gain rank in the Spirit by how available we choose to be to Him.

We see a lot of frustration in the church because there is so much unnecessary comparison and wrong perception. We treat one prophet or one singer one way, and another prophet and singer another. God is no respecter of persons. Everything He does is good, and we must reprogram our thinking to be in awe of everything God does through anybody at any given time.

My closing point here is, don't love the gifts more than the giver. What Jesus communicated to us above all was an extraordinary intimate relationship with the Father, and because of it, the Father was able to do extraordinary things through Him. We are to expand the kingdom. That happens as we draw close to Him and then execute what He tells us to do. I am all for the amazing miracles Jesus did, and I will not limit God out of fear. I will live in expectancy of His ability to perform through me however He chooses, but someone needs to obey God and write the movie, open the school, start the business, open the bank, audition, etc. He deploys us in amazing ways everywhere.

The enemy controls every facet of earthly life broken down into the following categories: religion, business, education, government, media, entertainment, and marriage and family. If everybody is healing the sick and raising the dead, how does that impact government? What if I am an artist? I have been in services where artists worship though painting and it has always been so powerful. What if someone, in the face of imagery that is historically rooted in supremacy, was called to birth out artwork that would allow others to identify with the real identity of Christ? That would be defeating a demonic agenda to keep God's people from Him. God can and will use us anywhere, and trust me, He will be sure to get the glory and make sure it ties back to Him. Expand the kingdom by complete submission and obedience to Him, and don't limit Him or minimize anything He tells you to do.

What we see from Genesis to Revelations is an emphasis on relationship not works alone. Works are used in demonstration to inspire and foster relationship. Works are not be worshipped.

Chapter Reflections

1. As you consider the life Jesus lived and the authority He demonstrated, what concerns you most about your ability to perform as He did and to do greater?

2. What inspired you about the transfiguration Jesus experienced?

3. Recap what you learned about ascension and descension. How do you see it impacting your relationship with God?

CHAPTER FIVE

Deployment: I am a Word out of God's Mouth!

"

"I knew you before I formed you in your mother's womb. Before you were born I set you apart and appointed you as my prophet to the nations." Jeremiah 1:5 NLT

When God gave me the revelation of deployment, it opened my eyes to Him and to my identity in an entirely new way. This is where it gets exciting. We have looked at the wonder of God through creation, the fall of man, the fall of Satan, and the violent interruption to Satan's plan with the introduction of Jesus into the earth, and we touched on how Jesus' intimate connection with the Father allowed Him to do extraordinary things that we now have the authority to do. We will touch on this authority more throughout the next few chapters, so here I want to focus on the notion of deployment and how from that understanding we should begin to see ourselves.

We are familiar with the term deployment through military usage of it, and as we have discussed that we were born into a holy war, it is befitting that God would inspire us this way. From the prophets of old up to Jesus, and now you and I, God has been as actively involved in our redemption as Satan has been in His attempts to keep mankind from it. So again keep the thought in mind here that from the deception of man to the resurrection and still today, there is an active war going on and we must take our rightful positions in it. Don't let that thought scare you; it will all make sense to you, I promise.

A Look at Military Deployment

Deployment is *the movement of troops or equipment to a place or position for military action.* It is *the action of bringing resources into effective action.* Prior to being called for deployment, one must be either drafted or must voluntarily enlist. Enlistment is not a given. In order to join the military, you must be a citizen or resident alien, you must be of a certain age (maturity), you must undergo a medical and physical examination to ensure mental and physical stability, and you must have a high school diploma. Things that can cause you to be rejected would be not meeting the above standards and/or having a criminal record.

Once successfully enlisted, recruits go into what is called basic combat training, also known as boot camp. Boot camp is said to be grueling and is not unlike what you see on television. Preparing for war is not supposed to feel like a trip to the spa. It is meant to break you down but strengthen you at the same time, and to condition you for any upcoming battle. It's meant to condition your mind for the "game." Recruits are put through strenuous physical activity to ensure they are in the best shape for whatever lies ahead, they are taught basic survival skills through being tested in some of the worst conditions, they are taught shooting, and they are taught to march. Marching may seem pointless, but it definitely has its place. To effectively march, the unit must be in synch and step together. In real live combat, where booby traps and bombs are planted, one misstep could kill an entire unit. Basic training is meant to turn civilians into soldiers.

Deployment is not easy. In fact it is quite disruptive. But once basic combat training is complete, one must be stationed wherever it has been decided. Deployment can mean leaving your family such as your spouse and children, communication with the outside world and those you love can be extremely limited—lasting for months at a time on occasion. It is a complete disruption to life as you knew it in exchange for stepping into the unknown and preparing to fight a battle you had nothing to do with initiating. Why do it? Most do so because they feel a responsibility to serve and protect their homeland. They pledged themselves to protecting their country of citizenship or residency, because they value it, because they have loved ones that live there, and there are a host of other reasons people decide to serve.

In addition to deployment, recruits can look to military advancement, which is a change in their ranking. There are 13 enlisted Army ranks: Private, Private Second Class, Private First Class, Specialist, Corporal, Sergeant, Staff Sergeant, Sergeant First Class, Master Sergeant, First Sergeant, Sergeant Major, Command Sergeant Major, and Sergeant Major of the Army. This varies depending on what branch of the military one chooses. But these positions are earned based on demonstrated capability, competence, relationship with officials above them, and experience. If one is going to pledge themselves to service, they may as well aspire to ascend as much as they can.

The purpose of war itself is unsettling, but it is something countries choose. It is always absolutely a choice, as there always other ways to resolve things. Though chosen, it is sometimes inevitable. The use of lethal force is carried out to push an often political agenda or to combat an invasion. Whatever the reason, once a war is on, everyone must be in position to do their part, and they must remember all that they learned in basic training and apply it, otherwise the possibility of death is quite high.

In Biblical times, war was also inevitable whether jealous cousins, punished for their rebellion, were attacking the Israelites or the Israelites were initiating a war to take the territory, it was necessary. We may not like the concept of war, but God in His infinite wisdom rendered judgment, and all that *He* does is just.

As you were reading about the military, its induction process, what deployment is, what the different rankings in military positions are, and about the disruption that deployment is to life as recruits know, you may have noted that there are quite a few similarities or parallels to what it looks like in comparison to the war of the realms. I'd like to explore these comparisons/similarities further.

God's Recruits & The Notion of Free Will

First, not everybody is chosen for recruitment. Just as the military has its requirements, so does God. The definition of deployment was noted as the movement of troops to a place or position for military action. Not everybody qualifies. We often assume that God created every human in existence. That is not so. Remember God had a divine will for creation that we discussed at length when we reviewed His original intentions. When man fell into the trap of sin, all other coming men were free to operate of their own free will. Genesis 3:15 notes Satan has seed as well.

Let's quickly define free will. I know we have labeled it as man's right to choose, and that is accurate. From God's perspective though, free will is what it meant to Him back in the Garden—"Choose ye this day whom you will serve." That's it. When we accept salvation, we have made our choice. We chose God. What we do that is out of alignment with His will for us is disobedience (sin) either knowingly or ignorantly. Because we belong to Him, we are brought back into correct alignment by conviction, which comes through the Holy Spirit.

One who has chosen a life without God has also made his decision. If you are not serving God, you've chosen to serve Satan. That may sound extreme because we assume serving Satan looks like demonic activity such as worshipping him (giving him adoration), demonic rituals, and whatever else comes to mind. But here is the reality; your life is going to be influenced by one of the two sides in the spirit realm. All humans have a spirit and that spirit will answer to something. A person that is not yielded to God and guided by the Word and the Holy Spirit are given over to their own lusts and their own understanding, which we know resists the perfect will of God and was never God's intention for man. One does not have to put Satan on display to serve him. The rejection of God alone gives Satan ownership of them, and that's what he craves—to be his own god with his own kingdom. Salvation reestablishes God's ownership of us by our choice.

We assume that engaging in sin is also the definition of free will. One could argue that you are technically acting of your own accord, but that is not how God defines it. His definition is more important than anything we can construct about it.

Another reason this understanding matters is because of the association we give free will with repentance. Hence, we must also define repentance. The Hebrew word for repentance is *shuv*, which is the root word of *Teshuvah*. It shows up nearly 1000 times in Hebrew Scriptures and means return or returning to God. We see it first occur in Genesis 3:19:

> *By the sweat of your face you shall eat bread, till you return to the ground, for out of it you were taken; for you are dust, and to dust you shall return.*

Remember we said God's definition for free will is "Choose ye this day whom you will serve?" Eve listened to Satan, convinced Adam to do the same, and therein their choice was made. They literally chose the knowledge of good and evil over God. At that point there was a renouncing—a shift in relationship and they were expelled from the Garden to go and live as they had chosen, and sin is in the world today. Up from the dust of the ground Adam was formed, and back to it he had to return. Judgment by God had been rendered. God explained to Adam that the day he ate of the tree he would surely die. God never said he would die instantly, He just said he would die. The *process* of death began immediately, but Adam lived 930 years and was responsible for the creation of humankind. The fall of man had catastrophic consequences. Because of it, all human life after him is born plunged into rebellion and sin.

Adam and Eve made their choice. They chose eternal death. We see from this example, an example of free will as a choice of whom to serve, not just the simple notion of a sin. Their decision was indeed sinful but it was more about the choice. They renounced God in that action. While we can speculate, given that in chapter 4 life seems to go on and God continues to provide for them, and we see sacrifices are being made to God by their sons, we have no biblical account of repentance on their part (repentance here meaning their turning back to God). God allowing Adam to live as long as He did was at His discretion.

Another Hebrew word for repentance is nacham, and it means to express remorse and/or to comfort oneself. Remorse here is regret and we see it also used in the New Testament. Remember that little lesson I gave you on exegesis? Here is another reason it *matters*.

> *And it repented the LORD that he had made man on the earth, and it grieved him at his heart. Genesis 6:6*

> *And the LORD said, I will destroy man whom I have created from the face of the earth; both man, and beast, and the creeping thing, and the fowls of the air; for it repenteth me that I have made them. Genesis 6:7*

Here we see God expressing sorrow and remorse; or one might say grave disappointment. Did God sin? Absolutely not! He is holy. There is no sin in Him. This definition appears several other times in the Old Testament and each time it speaks to some form of remorse (a search of Strong' s H5162 will bring up every text where the word is used either as remorse or comfort in deep sorrow. It is highly recommended that you research it).

When the word *shuv,* which is the root word of *Teshuvah,* is used in the texts, it is to "return," as we have established. It is man's destiny and duty to be with God. Living in His Presence with Him as our God forever was His intention. This notion of "returning" to that destiny and duty is to become aware of our transgression, to become aware of what we lost at the fall of man in other words, and choose to be restored to that state of being. It is moving from one state of being into the next, the next being restored to our original position. That is the free will choice of salvation. When God was imploring through the prophets for the children of Israel to repent, it was often in this context. The issue was not their actions as much as it was their hearts. Over and over again, God mentions that they are stiff necked and their hearts are from Him. They were making a conscious decision not to make God their God. An entire generation died out during the exodus because none of them were ever going to choose God, as He required it. He was their God in name only, but not the God of their hearts. And we see this same condition of heart throughout much of the Old Testament and into the New.

There is a difference between engaging in sinful activity and completely renouncing God and having a heart that is far from Him. Peter denied Jesus because he gave into fear, not because he did not love Him. Jesus understanding that restored Peter to his rightful place. When you have done something you know displeases God, are you truly stating that you want God no more and your choice is to rock with the devil from now on? For some that is the case. However, for most of us, it is not. We do love God, there's just something in our character that needs to be addressed. That does not dismiss us completely from salvation. Thank the Almighty God!

Religion has been known to collapse the two meanings of repentance and assume that one is backslidden every time they fall into a sinful trap. If that were true, who of us would be saved? We would all have to give our lives again to Christ every week or every day. There are some things that are harder to break—strongholds, and we are convincing people that they are in a backslidden state when they are not. Want proof? Ok!

Backsliding also known as falling away or committing **apostasy**, is a term used within Christianity to describe a process by which an individual who has converted to Christianity reverts to pre-conversion habits and/or lapses or falls into sin, when a person **turns from** God to pursue their own desire.

Don't let the definition fool you. This speaks to **renunciation**. Apostasy is the abandonment of or renunciation of a religious or political belief. This is not a one and done. If I fall and I curse out my neighbor in a moment of lapse of good judgment, I did not backslide. If I find that I am consistently cursing out my neighbors, I have not backslidden if I have not renounced God in my heart. What I need is deliverance, the act of being rescued or set free from whatever has me behaving out of alignment. That is not the same as complete renunciation, and people do and have renounced God to turn to their own way or even another religion.

Religious emphasis on sin and the collapsing of the definitions have caused many to feel defeated. Before we can even get believers to believe that they are special, that they have power, and that they have authority and are called to great exploits, they must first be mentally reconditioned. We have made faith and relationship with God about works and earning Christ (and we are still getting to the point of deployment, trust me) and we inadvertently create a bunch of defeated believers who are actually already justified and victorious. If we can't perceive ourselves as liberated because of Christ, we will never see ourselves as deployable. That's exactly what Satan wants!

We tell people that every time they sin they put Jesus on the cross again. That notion comes from Hebrews 6:4-6 and is actually not even written about believers, it's written to unbelievers.

Hebrews 6:4-6 states, "*It is impossible for those who have once been enlightened, who have tasted the heavenly gift, who have shared in the Holy Spirit, who have tasted the goodness of the word of God and the powers of the coming age and who have fallen away, to be brought back to repentance.*" I would argue this is one of the Bible's most difficult passages to interpret, but one thing is clear—it does not teach that we can lose our salvation (backslide) for sins we commit alone.

The text refers to unbelievers who are convinced of the basic truths of the gospel but who have not placed their faith in Jesus Christ as Savior. They are intellectually persuaded but spiritually uncommitted. We see this all the time. There are many we come across who know about God, who know about faith, who know about the crucifixion, and who may even know the Word but do not want salvation for whatever their reasons may be. These people have received enlightenment (truth and instruction) but understanding the Word or having knowledge, or even considering yourself spiritual is not the same as being regenerated by the Holy Spirit.

I remember feeling defeated by faith. No matter how hard I tried there was always some struggle here or there. I knew that I had accepted salvation. I knew that I truly loved God. I knew that I wanted more of Him. I knew that I wanted to serve Him. I made myself available to all of that as much as I knew how. Early on in life I was prostituted, molested, and raped almost daily for a season, and from that, because of what I was exposed to, I developed an addiction for pornography, masturbation, and became somewhat loose with my body. My actions had nothing to do with my not wanting to serve God. Of course I did. But I was judged and made to believe by some people that I couldn't possibly love God and be in that kind of sin. I had to make a choice. I understood the making a choice part from the standpoint of turning away sexual perversion. I just didn't know how to break what I would later learn was a generational curse and a stronghold. I felt weak and incapable and ultimately like a fraud. I buried myself in secret shame, which led me into a greater state of rebellion. My feelings of defeat borne out of ignorance and misinterpreted scripture led me to believe it was impossible to live holy and I found myself resigning myself to just being a failure at it. I could use my talents in the church, but beyond that there was no hope for me.

That feeling of hopelessness led me away from building a relationship with God and onto some dangerous and destructive paths, because I could not see how it was possible to live a holy life. Not in the way it had been described. How could I come to Him? I was too messed up. Surely He would be offended at my even approaching Him, I thought, so it was easier to ritualistically do church and operate in my gifts without coming too close. He was presented to me a Holy God waiting to catch me in sin and punish me, so it was best to hide from Him like a child avoiding a spanking.

A mistake every now and then was acceptable to most. One could just say sorry and get back up. But a mistake over and over again was a choice, and thus a sign of willful disobedience and being a horrible person in a wicked state. If I saw myself that way, and there are so many that I talk to who feel this way secretly (no matter what mask they put on), how was I ever going to qualify to be worthy of God's use? In no way am I dismissing sin. I am a firm believer in Holiness, and yes repentance *both* contexts. I do come to God in great sorrow and remorse when I become aware of my failures and ask for forgiveness, because I love Him.

However, I want to release someone from that religious state of mind. I am talking to sheep, evangelists, prophets, pastors, apostles, teachers, and believers of all titles and levels in their faith. I cancel the assignment of the strong hold of religious construct that keeps you in a state of disillusionment about who you are. Be released now from every place where condemnation has won in you. We declare for you an encounter that will move you from shame into liberty, and from liberty to deployment. I declare Romans 8:1 over your lives.

Don't you dare think that you are worthless and no better than a nonbeliever or one who chooses his own path. As we deal in just a few moments with you being a word out of God's mouth, your connection with your identity in God should become clearer to you if you receive it. You are qualified to serve by way of Christ on the cross, His resurrection, and your acceptance of Him as Lord of your life. The same as He defeated death, so did you when you made God your choice. You too got up from eternal death and stepped into eternal life in resurrection power, and you deserve to rejoice in that. There is no earning it, there is only cultivating it. Let's keep going.

So we assessed free will, and that led us to dealing with some necessary information that had to be stated so that you could be mentally freed up enough to receive al that we have yet to explore, but from all of the above stated, the point we have been building up to is that not all were put here by God. Many are born because of the choice to lay with another and that produced a baby. It was never their destiny to serve God, but God has pledged to make Himself available to all people. Nobody can say they have never heard of the gospel of Christ. What they do with that information is on them.

Those of us that become believers do not do so as a surprise to God. He is not up in Heaven saying, "Whoa, I did not expect Rein to give her life to Me, let Me figure out what to do with her." If God knows all, and He does, then you were always meant to be restored to Him, and He knew it before you were formed in the womb. We shall prove that in a moment. You are a work of His hand. The works of His hands are good. Despite all that you had to sift through whether you were religiously locked into seeing yourself as a wretch undone instead of a glorious extension of God in the earth saved by grace, or you had a different kind of collision with eternity meeting time that brought you to Him, you were always meant to, and you were qualified for service and deployment before you left the womb. Satan has his soldiers so to speak, and God most assuredly has His in every generation.

The God, our God who lives in Eternity and is Eternal and is All, knew from the formation of the earth to it's coming end of it as we know it has known every being that would inhabit it down to the number of hairs on their head, and His will for those that would believe and serve Him and make Him their Lord were chosen and planned for at "Come, let us make man in our own image," and perhaps well before even then. He always knew you—every aspect of you and your life were always known to Him. He saw you as He dwelt outside of time and entered into time as a part of Himself to take to a cross with you and your future on His mind. You may not feel like you are worthy to serve, but He does, and knowing your entire life from its beginning to end He created and released you into the earth for what you would eventually become. You are absolutely worthy to serve. If you were not, He would never have wasted the time. Again, I am talking about those of us who were predestined to make Him our God and walk it all the way.

Citizenship

Those who are to serve God become kingdom citizens through Jesus Christ. Most every person is born a citizen of a political state or country where they have identity, rights, protections, and share in a certain culture, morals, and values. Additionally, we are told in the Bible that each person is also born into the kingdom of this world where Satan rules (2 Corinthians 4:4) and is therefore enslaved as a member of that culture, taking part in Satan's values and practices—namely rebelling against God (Romans 6:16; Genesis 3:2, 1 John 2:16).

This is the sin we are born into and remain captives of until we are rescued and redeemed by Jesus (Ephesians 2:1-5). When we join the kingdom of God through the grace of Jesus and the power of His resurrection, our citizenship is transferred from the world ruled by Satan to the heavenly kingdom ruled by God (John 3:3;)Philippians 3:18-21 describes this concisely:

> "For many, of whom I have often told you and now tell you even with tears, walk as enemies of the cross of Christ. Their end is destruction, their god is their belly, and they glory in their shame, with minds set on earthly things. But our citizenship is in heaven, and from it we await a Savior, the Lord Jesus Christ, who will transform our lowly body to be like his glorious body, by the power that enables him even to subject all things to himself."

Maturity

As we walk out our faith life, we find that we are constantly maturing and growing, so there is no suggestion here that we must be fully matured in God in order to serve, whatever that tends to mean to us. So many are hesitant to step into what they feel compelled by God to do because they feel they aren't ready or aren't educated enough, or aren't mature enough solely based on their own reasoning and whatever that reason is influenced by. I have certainly been there.

By maturity, I take the liberty here of considering it as "set time." God has never been unaware of when we would come to the place of having an encounter with Him post salvation. After I received salvation, I understood I had many gifts, and I certainly grew up using every one of them in the church, but there would be a "set time" when I would have a collision with Eternity that would point me toward my destiny. At the point in which we encounter God in this way, we are also meeting a qualification for enlistment and eventually deployment.

Examination & Disqualification

Examination is another prequalification. God simply knows our heart through and through. He knows who will go all the way with Him and who will defect to another path.

Search (examine) me, O God, and know my heart (mind)! Try me and know my thoughts! Psalm 139:23

Examine me, LORD; put me to the test! Purify my mind and my heart. Psalm 26:2

As God examines the heart and mind, what "disqualifies" us if you will is His knowing who we are from our beginning to our coming end, and He knows in His infinite wisdom whose heart will remain far from Him. Additionally, one cannot "enlist" before making the choice to do so.

"Basic Combat Training"

Those of us that have ever been through a real process with God definitely understand the concept of spiritual boot camp. Much like in the military, boot camp is meant to break you down but strengthen you at the same time, and to condition you for any upcoming battle. Our will must first be traded in for His. Our mind must be reconditioned to think like He does. The process of transformation is not always easy. What puts a demand on the submission of our flesh, our will, and our desires we may find to be quite difficult or even painful. We will revisit this in our chapter on the process.

> *For the mind that is set on the flesh is hostile to God, for it does not submit to God's law; indeed, it cannot. Romans 8:7*
>
> *Humble yourselves, therefore, under the mighty hand of God so that at the proper time he may exalt you 1 Peter 5:6*

Deployment

When God deems us ready, we will receive orders from Him and will be positioned by Him to carry those orders out. I am using military language intentionally, but we also refer to His instructions as assignments. This is not a one and done. As we make our home in His presence, we avail ourselves to so much more of Him. The more of Him we get becomes the more of Him we can give out. He can use us for service as much as we open ourselves up to Him.

Ranking

The military ranks its officers from the lowest office of entry to the highest office of command as we said earlier. There are also spiritual rankings. We don't all carry the same ranking in the Spirit, that's solely up to God. We do not all start at the same place, and again, that's at God 's discretion, but advancement in Him is always available just by the continuation of availing ourselves to Him. Advancement in Him will cost us something. Some authority He freely gives us at His discretion, and some authority we earn by being willing and staying willing to live in His presence whatever it takes.

It is important to remember that God deploys us as He sees fit, we should not covet someone else's file or assignment or assume that our position is invaluable. Everything that God asks us to do as we said earlier is important. Wherever He places us and whatever the assignment, there is a need for it, and you are the right person for it. Our primary focus is hosting God and allowing Him to be God through us at all times. Remember it is not tenure that somehow makes us more advanced, that's man's standards. It is availability to God and God's decision alone on what He uses you to do.

God can raise us up very high in an instant or walk us slowly toward advancement. It's all left up to His wisdom. As I mentioned earlier, I have known those who call themselves master prophets based on their time and experience, and God has said, "Their hearts are from me." One can work a gift. Gifts from God are given freely. The more we use that gift, the better we get at it, God is not looking for a gift exchange. He wants relationship with Him that leads beyond the gifts, beyond even the anointing, and into the glory. We will discuss the glory of God in a later chapter.

Deployment is disruptive

Truthfully, a real encounter with God before you can be deployed is disruptive. Life as you knew it is forever changed. There will be some costs and things and people that we must let go of for the greater good. Even in knowing this, God is a reassuring and comforting God who stays right by our side every step of the way. Anything that we give up for Him and His purposes for us, He will always replace with better and even more. We see that example below as we consider Job and how He was chosen to be tested.

Drafted into holy war

Again, thanks to the fall of Satan in his arrogance and his deceptive plot against man and attack against God's throne, he started this war, and we have been enlisted into doing our part in finishing it. Satan's primary concern is to continue to raise his fist against God's throne in order to hold on to his empire here on earth, and God's primary concern is to restore us back to His original intention. We know in the end Satan loses, but we still must do our part down through the generations to recapture as much of dominion and territory as we can. We must be all God desires us to be in the earth to expand kingdom citizenship as much as possible before the return of Christ.

I want to state this very clearly, we should not under any circumstances fear Satan. He is cunning and he hits below the belt indeed through fear, deception, and distraction, but he is smoke and mirrors. He has no authority to kill you. If he did, every believer would be dead. He works over time in all kinds of messaging to make us see him as more powerful than he is, but he is limited in his strategy to come against you and he knows it.

Consider Job:

There was a man named Job, living in the land of Uz who worshiped God and was faithful to him. He was a good man, careful not to do anything evil. He had seven sons and three daughters, and owned seven thousand sheep, three thousand camels, one thousand head of cattle, and five hundred donkeys. He also had a large number of servants and was the richest man in the East.

Job's sons used to take turns giving a feast, to which all the others would come, and they always invited their three sisters to join them. The morning after each feast, Job would get up early and offer sacrifices for each of his children in order to purify them. He always did this because he thought that one of them might have sinned by insulting God unintentionally.

When the day came for the heavenly beings to appear before the LORD, *Satan was there among them. The* LORD *asked him, "What have you been doing?"*

Satan answered, "I have been walking here and there, roaming around the earth."

"Did you notice my servant Job?" the LORD *asked. "There is no one on earth as faithful and good as he is. He worships me and is careful not to do anything evil."*

Satan replied, "Would Job worship you if he got nothing out of it? [10] You have always protected him and his family and everything he owns. You bless everything he does, and you have given him enough cattle to fill the whole country. [11] But now suppose you take away everything he has—he will curse you to your face!"

"All right," the LORD *said to Satan, "everything he has is in your power, but you must not hurt Job himself." So Satan left.*

As you read the passage, it may seem cruel on the part of God to offer up Job like that, but remember I told you to keep in mind throughout the book that this is a holy war from the beginning of man's existence to present. Satan is fighting for a kingdom and to be God. God is simply responding. As you keep this notion of deployment in mind, you'll see every text in that light, and value everything God does throughout the Bible. This is a war that is a series of battles for both the redemption and the destruction of man, with Satan obviously on the side of our demise.

Job was a battle Satan initiated because He wanted to challenge God once again. In his arrogance and desperation he picks a fight he cannot possibly win. Still he is an agitator and he knew at the time that if he could get Job to curse God and die, without an effective atonement plan in place, it would be score one for Satan. Job, if you will, was a deployment and a lesson for us. He was enlisted to demonstrate unrelenting commitment despite the worst circumstances, and would be greatly rewarded for it. God knew His heart. You should know that God would never deploy you for an assignment you are not equipped for. And He certainly will not throw you into a battle you cannot win. Sometimes *you* may discover who you are as you go, but God is not in the process of discovery with you. He *knows* whom you are through and through and what He built you for.

And to address any fear of stepping out, note that God maintained control over Satan. He does not have the free reign we assume that he does. God grants him the liberty of some powerful torment for Job, no doubt, but he does not give Satan permission to kill Job. Satan cannot do any more to you than God will allow. At best he can try to deceive you into self-destruction by trying to poison you against God through lust, pride, distraction, fear, or whatever he can use to steal your attention away from God. No weapon formed against you [when you belong to God] has authority to prosper or prevail over you. Warfare may look like it's winning as it did for Job, but God is the Master at offering the way of escape. We see even for Job and all his crises, he still emerges victorious and doubly blessed. Victory is always your portion no matter the battle, as long as you are working with God and not against Him.

You are a Word.

When God in His goodness and loving kindness ministered this to me, I had to really sit with Him about it. It wasn't that I didn't believe Him, I just had to take it all in, picture it, and then digest it. Sometimes in the Bible, another name for Jesus is the Word. I am not referring to that. I am referring here to God's creative word.

Nine times, "And God said..." appears in Genesis chapter 1. Each time God spoke that, something was formed, created, or made. The worlds came into being, were beautifully coordinated and now exist under the complete command of God.

> *Hebrews 11:3, "Through faith we understand that the worlds were framed by the Word of God..."*

God's word is full of creative energy, power and life. When God created anything, He used His word like a builder wields his hammer and tools. When He speaks a thing, what leaves His mouth is commanded to do His bidding.

By His word the oceans know how far to caress the shore. By His word the stars retain their positions in the cosmos. By His word light rolled back the darkness that covered a void and formless earth. By His word, all sea life came into being and their habitat stretches from nation to nation. By His word, the flowers bloom and a seed in the ground breaks open in order to break out of the ground and stretch up toward heaven with the audacity to provide us something edible and for our nourishment along the way. By His word first, then His Hand, and with His breath man became a living soul.

Familiarity breeds contempt. We said earlier in our chapter on apathy that we have become so desensitized to the wonders of God all around us. When we see His creations as common, we tend to treat Him as common. We are not common with Him. Losing our awe for Him and the mighty works of His hands is often what keeps us from seeing ourselves as anything more than a poor wretched soul. I believe that offends Him because all that He created is good.

I remember when I had my first child. I was filled with a sense of both amazement and fear. I was amazed (despite the morning sickness, swollen feet, back pain, and eventual labor pain) that an entire life could be growing inside me. I became so aware of the human body and how every organ has a specific function, and how creative God even was in the man carrying a seed and my womb being an incubator. As my baby grew, things moved around, but my body automatically knew how to accommodate the changes. My breasts new to prepare for milk, my body knew to store fat, the baby connected to my feeding system and was nourished, and even in the release of the baby's fluids, my system was not poisoned. If I got sick, my body fought it. I was amazed at how the body preserves itself, and even more amazed to release a baby boy, a part of me into the earth. It was astounding that this precious baby came out of my belly. He was mine, and he was so perfect in every way.

I imagine God feels the same, I imagine that He looked out at all of His handy work, and not only declared it good, but admired it and smiled at it, and wanted the best for it all. His word is not worthless. Everything He created has its own unique purpose. Study the life of bees and you'll have an entirely new respect for flowers, honey, and pollination. Consider how majestic the lion and the elephant are, or how amazing the giraffe. I had a chance to go on an African Safari during my time in ministry there, and my son and I were almost in tears to behold God's creations in their natural habitats. When we stop admiring His creations, we stop often stop admiring *Him*. His word imparts power and creates life. His word is a lamp, His word is truth, His word is above, and His word is living and active.

His word also spoke *you* into existence. We seem to believe that we are here because our parents laid together, and as we accept salvation, it's at that point that God decides to actually do something with our life, if we ever actually seek for what that is. It's often not until later in life that we even stop to contemplate the meaning of life. We live apathetically to any involvement in a possible higher future or greater meaning for our lives. Religion has taught us to avoid hell at all costs, serve the church faithfully, find something to do in the church, and outside of church we live a separate life of work, school, marriage, and family, intent on trying to fill our lives with whatever we feel is missing. Listen, prior to man's fall, the only thing to do was bask in the presence of God and enjoy the wonders of the world He created for us. Post man's fall, life for us shifted completely. Not only do we have to find our way to the presence of God (and sometimes fight our way thanks to opposition), we also have to deploy. We have to carry God back into the earth. You're not going to discover God's will for your life sitting on a pew doing the same old thing and engaging in half hearted attempts at a prayer life. You are more than that. You are a word out of God's mouth that is meant to be a harvest to Him. Listen to what He says to Jeremiah.

"I knew you before I formed you in your mother's womb. Before you were born I set you apart and appointed you as my prophet to the nations." Jeremiah 1:5 NLT

Check that out! God Himself visits Jeremiah (encounter) and says, "I knew you (relationship) before I formed you (creation) in your mother's womb." In other words, Jeremiah had a relationship with God or God had a relationship with Jeremiah before God formed Him in the womb. Jeremiah could have been in spirit relationship with God, or He could have been a thought in His mind, but at some point, like God did with Adam, He spoke Jeremiah and formed Him. God takes ownership of Jeremiah as His formation and works it like He did Jesus through a womb to be deployed into the earth at the right time for God's intended purpose, not just for Jeremiah, but for the nation and people Jeremiah would have to be deployed to.

God didn't just form Him without a plan. He follows up by saying, " I set you apart." I had a plan and a blueprint, I made a decision about what I would use to do and where I would use to do it. I enlisted you and deployed you to be a prophet to the nations! Whoa!

In *one* encounter, Jeremiah learns God as creator and that He is an intentional and unique creation himself, he learns he is a chosen vessel, and he is made aware of his identity in God, which shifted from one state of being into another— destiny. How awesome is that? We make it more difficult than it needs to be. Clearly Jeremiah, even as a young person in training possessed the right heart for God and found Himself in the presence of God so that God could fill him up with a revelation of God Himself, a revelation of who he was to be in God, and a deployment.

When we spoke of Jacob's ladder we talked about ascension and descension and carrying God into the earth. This is exactly what happened with Jeremiah. It will not look the same for all of us. Jeremiah knew he had to prophesy to the nations. You and I may have to prophesy with our life on a different mountain in a different way. We will talk about mountains later.

It is important to value the Word of God more than we often do. When God said, "Let there be light," light didn't say, "No Lord, I want to be a rainbow." The Word out of the mouth of God couldn't resist God. Catch that! Light came forth and was the electrons, photons, reflection, and energy it needed to be. God spoke the word light alone, but light produced every aspect of what God saw in His mind when He said it.

You as a true word out of the mouth of God cannot resist God either.

> So shall my word be that goeth forth out of my mouth: it shall not return unto me void, but it shall accomplish that which I please, and it shall prosper in the thing whereto I sent it. Isaiah 55:11

You are a Word that has left His mouth, that travelled into a womb, that came through a birth canal specifically to accomplish whatever God pleases, and catch this, you shall prosper in the thing He sends you to. That's not God saying *maybe* you will. That's a promise to you and a whole threat to the enemy! Those are both producing and fighting words!

You are not satisfied where you are because the Holy Spirit is pushing you to a higher place. There is an awakening now happening in your spirit man to obey the unction to discover what it is you must become. You may as well deploy! You have no choice. His word does not return to Him void or as a failure...**ever**. Seeing yourself in this way changes everything. You are Word that shall produce and prosper as you do. Go find out what the enemy is terrified of you knowing.

And just like light, everything you are to become, God didn't have to speak individually. He said your name, and everything He knows you are to be and intended for you to produce, every infinite thought He had about you, every possibility in you, and as far as you will go in Him was embedded in your DNA. The enemy doesn't want you to ever discover it, but the Holy Spirit's job is to lead you right to it. Quench not the spirit! Why?

You are a deployment.

Not only are you a word out of His mouth purposed to achieve what He wants, you should consider yourself an assignment or deployment. You are an answer to something somewhere. God is addressing a groaning in the earth through your existence. Where a place is void of God, You shall introduce His presence there. Where the enemy is holding something hostage, you shall snatch it out if his possession.

When a war is about to take place, the general and the commanders and key officers (forgive me if I didn't get that right) come together to review the Intel on the enemy. The strategy for the defeat of that enemy is released, and those that receive the information must relay it and then make sure that it gets perfectly executed according to the way it was all laid out. No officer in charge has the authority (unless granted) to act independently or of his own accord. Not adhering to what has been laid out could cost soldiers their lives.

Jeremiah received clear instructions. He knew he would prophesy to the nations. His job was to say what God said to whoever God instructed him to say it to. He didn't have the liberty of speaking from the soulish realm. He was much too close to God for that. He had difficulty executing no doubt, but even He said, (paraphrased), if I try to contain it, it just burns hot within me, it's like fire, shut up in my bones. I can't not be what you intended. Why? Every word of God is an absolute.

Are there those that God will speak over who will fail? Absolutely. God knew that. For whatever reason they were given the space and opportunity to hear the truth and be enlightened and yet reject God. Hebrews 6 revealed to us earlier, there is no hope for these people. God's reasons for trying are His alone. We aren't talking about those people who serve as an example for us of what not to do. I am talking to God's deployments—His true deployments that He knows will go all the way, even when it gets hard, rough, painful, and you want to quit. The deployments He knows are devoted to Him and care about the things He cares about more than their own life, are the ones I am addressing. I am talking to you. Don't worry, I'll give you the steps later for how to develop this kind of relationship with God, but for now, just know, this means you.

Jonah tried to avoid deployment and found himself in the belly of a whale. God could have killed Him, but His word will never lie. Jeremiah wanted to shut up, but found it quite impossible. Daniel was purposed and obedient right into the lions den, but no harm came to him, Peter denied Jesus three times, but still found himself preaching the greatest revival ever and 3000 souls converted. Moses had to confront a relentless Pharaoh whose heart God himself hardened but eventually got the people set free.

There is no word God speaks, that a heart that is truly made for God can avoid. He made you with His mouth and infinite wisdom, and purpose will not miss you either. Even if it takes a jolt or a breaking and stripping as it admittedly did for me (and after a 10 year detour mind you), if God purposed in His heart for it to be **you** to carry a thing out, trust me, you will. I believe you have this book because He is talking directly to you no matter how long you have been saved or what your title may be. If there is more for you, you will walk it all.

God will love on you, share with you, test you, break your will, build you up, build your trust in Him, and do whatever is necessary in you and with you to ensure your success. All you have to do is show up to hear. He will do the rest.

Chapter Reflections

1. How does it shift your perspective of yourself to know that you are a word out of the mouth of God?

2. In what ways have you carried guilt or condemnation?

3. In what ways does the information in this chapter change the way you will seek God about your destiny?

CHAPTER SIX

Deployment: Every Assignment is a Battle Strategy

"

For consider your calling, brothers: not many of you were wise according to worldly standards, not many were powerful, not many were of noble birth. But God chose what is foolish in the world to shame the wise; God chose what is weak in the world to shame the strong.
1 Corinthians 1:26-27 ESV

We said earlier that every assignment matters. God deploys us to accomplish what He wants, and He owes no one an explanation. 1 Corinthians 1:26-27 reminds us that God chose what was foolish in the world to shame the wise, and what is weak in the world to shame the strong. We can never completely grasp all that God is doing because His ways and His thoughts are higher. We do well to just carry out His instructions, and whatever we are to understand we will usually understand it after its execution. What I want to stress to you in this chapter, is that no matter what it is God tells you to do, see it as a battle strategy. Remember we talked about the opening of the file and the Intel, and the strategy to defeat the enemy therein? What God gives us to do is essentially the same. Every Word He speaks has a much higher purpose than we often know. The seemingly littlest things that we obey can have the greatest impact for the kingdom. If you do one thing God tells you to do, and a soul gets saved, all of heaven rejoices. That's huge. It doesn't require a spotlight or grand stage all the time, but His instructions have lasting implications down through the generations, and serve as a death-dealing blow to the agenda of the enemy every single time.

I was convicted when God revealed this to me, because there were things I could immediately recall that He instructed me to do that I hadn't. This book was one of those deployments. I had this unction in 2012, here it is almost the end of 2020, and I am just writing it. Sure I could claim that I didn't quite have the fullness of the revelation that I have now, but there was no excuse for not seeking for it then. My apathetic nature caused me to delay. It is not that God was surprised that I would delay. Of course He knew. He also knew that I would get to this place of understanding and conviction and never take for granted what He tells me to do again. Knowing that all of His instructions carry kingdom implications, which ultimately wreck hell's plans gave me a new burning desire to position myself in the presence to receive more orders and execute them, because they matter to God and matter to kingdom. I refuse to be a useless soldier. I want to excel in carrying God into the earth by hosting Him and allowing Him to work through me, whatever the assignment. This is war! Whatever my part is in it, whatever your part is in it, we have the enemy in our sights, let's take the shot! Don't let the enemy escape still holding kingdom keys or anyone else hostage.

One deployment can change your entire life.

I want to share an assignment God gave me back in 2011 that completely altered my course, in hopes of demonstrating what obedience will accomplish in your life.

Several years ago I was engaged to the wrong man. Wrong is actually an understatement, I just can't seem to find the right words to articulate it. Things could always be worse for us, so my intent is not to glorify my struggle over anyone else's, but for me, in the fragile state I was in, it was bad. In my incessant need to be loved and because of my idolization of marriage, I let a man into my life and my children's lives that was simply full of the devil.

There's a detailed account of it all in the second installment of my life story "Redemption is Real," so I won't go into that too much here. The bottom line is this man was a liar, a manipulator, a thief, a drug addict, an undercover homosexual who also dealt in hetero and homosexual orgies, and to this day, I just thank God, that God loved me enough to shut it all down with my physical health in tact. Needless to say it ended, and in the worst publicly humiliating way. I had to retract the wedding invites, change my social media, and pretty much disappear from the public eye to lick my wounds.

If I thought things couldn't get any worse, life really hit a turning point for me. Not only did I have to deal with the pain, embarrassment, and public humiliation of the breakup, I had to face my children who were broken, angry, and gravely disappointed in me, and that threw me into a depression. I just couldn't function for a minute, so I missed a lot of work and lied about the reasons why. When I finally went into work, I was called into my boss' office and appropriately dismissed. You know I went numb. This was a high paying position that afforded us our lifestyle. I had no clue what I was going to do next. Even in the unknown, I remember understanding that God was clearly trying to get my attention.

I held on to the house with all that I had until I just had to admit I couldn't do it anymore. Having to move back into my mother's house in my 30s was the worst feeling ever. I had already let my children down enough. To have to uproot them was not a good feeling at all. I thank God that I had a place to go, but my life was falling completely apart. Nothing was in my control, and I was an emotional wreck with seemingly no direction, no prospects for a job, no money, and no hope.

My children couldn't take it. My two oldest got together and decided that they wanted to go live with their father. I was devastated. They didn't mean any harm, it was something they always wanted and something that he always avoided, but the timing couldn't have been worse. I raised them by myself all their lives from struggling to finally thriving with no support from their father for quite a while. We were often at odds back then, so I learned early to get my own plan in place so that I wouldn't have to depend on him. Over the years everything was my fault. No matter what I said or did, it was always twisted to make me look like the bad guy, so much so a lot of his family turned against me and treated me like I was the devil they had to sneak around. So for my children to choose to "abandon" me at my worst really hurt. They weren't actually abandoning me. That was my pain talking back then. I knew that they needed that time with him, and I didn't want to be responsible for keeping them from him. We did eventually grow out of the tug of war and managed to be cordial.

Just a few weeks after seeing them off, I was trying to figure out my mess of a life when my mom came home stating that she had a lump and it turned out to be stage 4 cancer. I was glad I was with her of course, that's my mom, but I cannot lie to you. While trying to assure her that all would be well (and it was thank God), I couldn't help yelling to the heavens from inside myself, "O come on!"

I knew that all of this was meant to draw me to my knees. I am not saying that God initiated it, that was all on me, and the rest, well life played it's part, but I could feel the pull to really turn to Him this time. I was down to nothing. There was literally nothing else to do.

When the instruction came to write " I am not Garbage," a very detailed encounter of my life growing up, I was not interested. First, who wants to expose their family issues like that? We are talking prostitution by my grandmother at 5 years old, being daily molested and raped or just shy of it, drug addiction, alcoholism, I mean yea... no! I did not want to even touch that. If I were going to write it, it would have to be after my mother passed. There was no way I could write and recall things I had never even told her let alone anyone else, and don't get me started on needing to completely avoid my porn addiction, masturbation addiction, poor relationship choices, that time I thought I was a lesbian, yea this was not happening. If God wanted me delivered, He was going to have to do so *privately*.

It really didn't help that during that season I kept getting prophetic word after prophetic word about my destiny. I promise I couldn't go anywhere without some random person speaking into my life about my future. I appreciated it, but what I really wanted was to be married. Back then I had a difficult time being alone, so in my mind I needed that sealed up before any kind of real ministry could start. I realize how crazy that sounds now. I was completely broken, with no purpose I knew of, asking God to allow me to avoid dealing with major emotional issues and skip me right into a marriage that was supposed to magically fix all my issues, and last how? Chile, I can't even tell you. It's just where I was.

God does not let up! Earlier I told you that when He purposes for you to do something, you will not get away from it. My church was having anniversary services, and Martha Munizzi, a well-known gospel-recording artist was the guest. I was asked to lead a song with the choir and reluctantly agreed. Of course she heard me sing, and of course that drew her attention to me, and of course God spoke to her about me, and of course she ministered to me publicly about becoming a prophet to nations. And yep, obey the instructions God just gave you. Sigh. To drive the nail in the coffin, she preached on David's life falling completely apart and his time of depression in the cave. I mean who can argue with that? I just wanted a husband. Then we could talk about all these great ministry exploits later.

I did obey. God assured me that my family would be covered and gave me the strategy for how to write the stories, and I got to work. I wish I could tell you it was easy. To be honest, I felt tortured. Having to pull up all these memories with such detail was a very dark and scary time for me. All I could do was get a chapter or a portion of one out and then go fall on my face before God to help me through.

Though it started very scary and painful, and though I didn't understand the necessity of writing this book and what it had to do with anything I was asking God for (such as putting my life back together maybe), it had the fortunate side effect of drawing me closer to God, and of transformation. Things I had buried deeply away in my soul were being exposed to the light, and as they were, for the first time in my life, I started to actually feel free. It became a time I looked forward to. The more I came before Him, the more chains broke off. Whatever chapter I was on, and whatever the story I was recalling, I actually started getting excited and operating in the expectancy that as soon as I was done, it was time to heal that too.

I cannot tell you how it shifted me out of religion and into relationship. I no longer felt afraid to come before God because He was showing me it was safe, and that He wasn't just waiting for me to get close so He could tell me how horrible I was. I was feeling and embracing His love and starting to trust Him more. The next thing I knew, I looked up, and worship, the way He intended it, was a whole lifestyle. I spent so many days just in awe of what broke off, and how free I was to say my abusers names without breaking down, becoming ferociously angry, or completely withdrawing. It started out uncomfortable, but the more I sat before Him, I began to understand that He initiated this life reset to set me on the right course for my life. He wasn't punishing me! Instead, He allowed all that I had to essentially crumble, just to expose me to myself in an entirely new way. I didn't know all that He had planned, but I knew greatness was on the other side. All I could think about was getting there.

By the time the book was published, printed, ordered, and shipped out, I was a completely different person. He had birthed in me this ministry of transformation and deliverance, and I was actively releasing everywhere I could what He had done for me, and how they could experience that same liberation.

I am not saying that it was not a process; I am not saying that I was always on point with the discipline. There were definitely days I wanted to look back, days I missed the money, days I just wanted to prove to my children that I was different. The enemy fought me every step of the way from trying to interfere with my writing, to sickness, to loneliness, to fear of even releasing the book. It was definitely a battle of wills, and I was smack dab in the middle.

As the book gained in popularity in my area, God ministered to me that He was going to use me to prophesy and reaffirmed international deployment. Now I had experienced the gift through others, and all I could think was, "Good God I am never going to get married (insert laughter or face palm here, you choose)." I was afraid. That declaration came with an entirely new demand on my life. I didn't feel worthy enough to prophesy to anybody or walk with that kind of gift.

A Christian woman who knew me in the area purchased the book, and she invited me to speak at one of her women's group sessions in her home. I brought it to my apostle and he cleared me to go. I did not want to be out here like some sort of uncovered vagabond. Preaching was not the issue. I have been doing that all my life. I just wasn't sure what to really expect. As he gave me the clearance to accept the invitation, he started ministering to me that God was going to do the extraordinary. Of course that scared me. But, with a lump in my throat, books in my trunk, and knees shaking I went and decided to let God be God. I knew that I had something to say and believed these women would be blessed by how God delivered me.

By the time I finished sharing, the women were broken before Him. I called a prayer line intending to just intercede (after all I got my start in the holiness church, I knew how to work an altar for sure). There were about 30 or so of us there, and as I began to pray and lay hands, I found myself prophesying, I was seeing pictures above their heads, for some of them their bedrooms and things He wanted said about the space, recalling events in their lives I could never have known, speaking to curses and casting out demons, it was crazy. Who was I? I grew up seeing it at the altar, but to be on that side was an entirely new world. I thought that it would take years to develop as a prophet (I actually did continue to develop and haven't stopped since), but God literally just opened my mouth. The gift wasn't just for special people. Here I was doing what I'd seen others do without any special training, and all I had to be was available for use. I was almost afraid it was a fluke, but there was literally a word for every woman in that room, and all testified that God indeed spoke. I was floored. I reported back to my apostle who told me to get ready for more.

Sure enough, my name started to spread like wild fire. I went from being someone nobody really knew outside of all the rumors about me, to seeing my face on flyers, and a phone that wouldn't stop ringing. I had no plan for this. I didn't have a team. It was just my youngest son, my mom, and I, and it was go time. The doors were flying open for me and many were getting healed, delivered, and set free, young and old alike. They were thanking me for my transparency and telling me I was a voice for their pain and liberty that they could never be. If I could paste a thousand crying emojis here I would. All this from a book?

The doors that opened for me didn't stop there. God said to the nations and He meant it. I barely comprehended what was happening to me in my local area in California, and now I was supposed to go from a few cities to whole other worlds?

A woman I was associated with was going to Italy to minister. She wanted some of us to give her some of our books to take with her. I was hesitant. The book was selling well and I really needed the money, so when God said sow 7, I said, "God that's $175.00 I need!" It's amazing how we can be involved in so many life-altering experiences with God and still be so low thinking. I laugh at myself now when I think about how I was complaining to an infinite God about $175.00.

God did not let up. I had to meet her at an event and carried the 7 books in my trunk. Of course I forgot to give them to her before we parted ways. I got home and thought, "Oh well, it wasn't meant to be." God on the other hand pushed me to find out where she would be next, and with less than $30.00 to my name for the gas, once again I had to drive just over two and a half hours praying that I would make it all the way there and back home. You never pray harder than when you have no money, miles and miles to go, and the needle is just about to kiss that "E." I made it there and back on nothing but the grace of God and pleading the entire way, but it was done. I was actually grateful to know that my book would be in the hands of 7 people in a foreign country. That was worthy of praise alone. Turns out I was the only one that adhered to the call for books, and the host (who would later become a great mentor and friend) ended up with a copy in her hands. She found me on Facebook and messaged me for a way to order more copies for the women's ministry. I was so excited. My book was going to be ordered and stocked in a bookstore for a church in Italy. Wow! I had never done any ministry out of my area at the time, not even in another state in the US, so to have my book there was a great way to experience ministering in another country whether in person or not. All I could do was thank God and thank my associate graciously for taking them.

To my surprise I received an inbox asking me for a time to call me, and as we talked I realized she was really inviting me to fly to Italy and minister for a conference. I must have pulled the phone away from my ear and looked at it like three times before I heard myself committing to pray with her about God releasing me to go. I remember thinking, "Now God I know you promised to raise me up, and you promised to send me out into the world literally, but this fast? Is this a mistake? Turns out it wasn't. By the time I heard back a few months later, the event was already fully planned, my itinerary was set, plane ticket paid for, hotel reserved, and by faith they just needed me to be available. I love how God works. My sister was graduating from college that May, and I remember like it was yesterday Him telling me not to plan anything else for that entire month and to wait for what He was going to do. I had no idea what to expect, but God told me to say yes, and it was set.

When I tell you we had a time, oh my goodness we did. They had several services planned and a weekend retreat booked. I was ready. I had been before God (largely because I was nervous), and I had the words to release. This was a different place for me. It wasn't about the book. This was the reestablishing of me as the preacher I once was before I detoured, and now it was time the prophet fully emerged. I walked in just expecting God to move every time. Move He did!

At every service including the retreat, we were completely drenched in the power and presence of God. He was prophesying, healing, and casting things out, restoring, breaking, singing, preaching, and miracle working. I had never done anything like that in my life to that magnitude of ministry. It was literally letting go and letting God. By the last Sunday that I would stand in that pulpit, we would literally go from 9am to almost midnight! I had no breaks, no water, no food, nothing. The church building was full because word had gotten around the military base that they had to come see this prophet God sent from the USA. Even other churches that had previously fellowshipped with the two churches hosting the event came with their members. The young people were leaving to go get their parents and friends so I could minister to them. There was no letting up. My God!

For hours God just had His way. Whatever He wanted to do, we sensed it and we did it. A lame man walked. I was spoken to in Italian and understood it in English, because the first few events were for the women, the husbands came in droves to receive, and receive they did. They were filled with the Holy Spirit, released into ministry, made aware of their destinies, had their marriages restored, wombs were prophesied to. God was just moving to give all of us an encounter whether you spoke English, an African language, Spanish, or Italian. We had so many moments where we had to just bend over in tears and adoration because everything God did was so profound. They wanted restoration and an encounter and by God they got it. I was forever changed after that week. We were so caught up, that they didn't want me to leave and extended my stay to minister one last time. That is nobody but God.

The doors didn't stop there either. God would later send me to the Philippines through China, and then to Africa, and every single time, it was the same experience as Italy and greater. Each new assignment released something new in me. In the Philippines we prophesied the rain to fall because they had been in major drought, we raised a woman up off her death bed until she was sitting up and praising God, we affirmed a church second location launch and led the ribbon cutting ceremony, we brought huge bags of rice to all the houses we could visit in the area and watched God perform miracles and healings as we went, and in Africa, it was just as powerful.

I told you that I really wanted to be married. It didn't happen right away. God was determined to establish and elevate me all over the world first, but assured me that it all had a purpose. He told me that if I just kept walking in obedience, I would look up and there my husband would be. He did not lie. After one of my ministry journeys to Africa, I was having a conversation with a long time Apostle friend, and it was in that conversation that God affirmed him as my husband. This man had demonstrated interested in me some 7 years earlier. I was still in my process, so I was very short, distant, and even kind of off-putting. I didn't think we were a good match. We were just so opposite. But who knew that 7 years later, in a conversation God led me to reach out to have, this same man would be the husband I had been craving?

God affirmed it for me, gave Him an encounter that threw him on his face in worship, and when he called me, he had an entire revelation from being in the presence of God. He knew all those years I was his wife, but he patiently waited and lived his life until I knew. We sought counsel to be sure and received confirmation after confirmation. It was ridiculous in a good way. Our friends would break into tongues and affirm the relationship before we could even get the words out good. After being completely assured, he proposed 4 days later and flew in to make it official and meet the family.

I know I shared a lot in that. I don't want to make it about me, or anything I received. It's not a selfish, self-centered testimony. I wanted to share this so that you could connect the dots between resistance, presence, transformation, obedience, and destiny. "I" did not do anything great on my own. God kept finding His way to me to restore me. When I finally yielded to committing to stay in His presence, He gave me an assignment. As I deployed by writing, He healed me every step of the way. By the time the book was done, I was an entirely different person with an entirely new identity. He then sent me out to release into the earth what He had done for me and put in me, and the more I stayed before Him became the more I knew Him. The more of Him I knew became the more of Him I could release into the earth.

I didn't have to fast 80 days, I didn't say 30 "Hail Mary's," I didn't speak in tongues or dance my way in. There was no religious formula that I could execute that made me suddenly worthy. I found my way into His presence, I obeyed His voice to write the book, and my entire life changed as I knew it. Guys... it all started with *a book*. Who but our God moves that way and shifts us into purpose like that? Where would I be today had I refused to obey the orders? How many people all over the world would have been deprived of an encounter with God through me? It's not that God needs me, it's that He chose me. And guess what? If he could choose an abused, broken, scared, withdrawn, confused, and discarded person like me, He can certainly choose you. I am not special in a superior since. I just found my way to Him and He did the rest. And He is still deploying me in a variety of ways to this day. Not everything is about preaching on a global stage before thousands of people. That experience has forever changed me, but I yet thank Him and am humbled by the private calls I get for prayer and He moves. I am grateful for the mentorship He allows me to offer and the ability to see lives change and people deploying. I am grateful for every prayer call I am asked to do, every zoom meeting (a video conference program), and every social media broadcast where there is no "fame," per se, no conference fee, and no big audience. I am grateful to be able to minister with my husband on a phone call or to a small group about marriage. I am grateful for every local church that has trusted my ear and invited me in for a release from God. I am humbled when He says, "Pray for that lady" as I am shopping in Walmart.

I used to believe that real ministry was done on a large scale, and that one must be really favored if God allowed them to have a mega church. My version of success was going all over the world to preach, and I did, but not before He changed my mindset. Sometimes we think that because we don't have a wider audience, we are not as valuable. In fact, move to critique something done by a leader with a large influence, and the response will almost always minimize and trivialize what *you're* doing as nothing.

Religion and the world at large have influenced us to conform to whatever standards it lays out, but if that is success, then why aren't we seeing more encounters with God? I am in no way criticizing or condemning large ministries. I expect that God is moving us toward one as well, but if we aren't being taught to see ourselves as necessary, as deployments, as kingdom, and how to live in the presence of God, then what on earth pray tell are we doing?

When God started shifting my life, I went from walking behind and alongside so many to walking up ahead. When that happens, you find out who is really truly for you. I didn't feel I was superior or any better, I just found my way to the presence and deployed. Whatever I heard I did. I gave up complete control, and God could then do whatever He wanted. Most of it was equally as surprising to me. While they were asking, "Why her?" I was literally asking the same thing, "Why me?" I didn't want the spotlight. I still don't do flattery or too much praise. The glory does not belong to me. It belongs to God. I am a complete introvert. Nobody knows how hard I work to tolerate being looked at live or on camera. It's just always been in my DNA from stage plays to pulpits to prophesying, to turn on, focus, and deploy. When I am done, I go back to my cave. I have found that many don't think I deserve anything more than they have, and just don't want it for me.

God would show me a particular sister in Christ who He would whoop over and over again, because no matter what He told her to do concerning me, she would never allow herself to obey. If I engaged in something larger scale, or if it seemed the deployments were booming, He would show me her folding her arms in frustration and anger. He showed me visions of her rolling her eyes about me in private and even allowed me in on some email conversations. He didn't show me to hurt me, He showed me to teach me and to make me aware. This is a given. Whenever you elevate, anybody around you that does not have a purified heart or a real identity in Him will feel slighted because somehow you moved up the road. Your moving up makes them aware they are still in the same place and afraid they're being left behind. A prideful heart cannot rejoice. Instead, they will judge, project, and even pridefully state that God is taking more time with them because He wants to do more with them. They are partially right. God would love to do more with them. The harvest is plentiful and the laborers are few, which means God is not holding anybody back who is ready. Readiness means living in His presence, not looking for man's elevation or seeding our way up. That kind of prideful attitude does not move God. He hates pride.

I shared this to demonstrate that this person has the wrong attitude. She wants to deploy, but she wants to do it her way, on her terms, based on her definition of what is most notable and valuable and gains her the accolades, though she says she doesn't want that. God can't deploy her or any of us who are attached to our deployment being packaged a certain way. I appreciate local ministry as much as I do International. I want the same encounter everywhere. Until we accept the lane God has carved out for us, we will be stuck right where we are.

He does not compete for control. Maybe you have been the target of someone feeling this way about you, or maybe, if you're willing to be honest, you are the bitter one. Either way, we all have a responsibility to live in the presence and deploy. There are far greater things to worry about, like all the people who remain in the clutches of the enemy and all the world systems he has influence over that affect us all. We shouldn't waste valuable time comparing our deployments to another's. We serve the same God. We are on the same team. The Sunday school teacher is just as important as the prophet. The smaller church (assuming it is one God dwells in) is no less important than the mega church God dwells in. I cannot state this enough. Your assignment is important. If it weren't God wouldn't waste His time.

I started with a book. There was nothing glamorous about that. It largely consisted of me bawling my eyes out on the floor and then being restored enough to write some more and doing it all over again. There was no spotlight on me. It was God and me. He decided to shine the light, I didn't. But that light didn't suddenly start shining when I stepped on a stage in Italy. It was shining in my room when God started setting me free. It was shining as I typed. It was shining as I shopped. It was shining in my home. We don't have to be a household name to be somebody 's answer. We just need right perspective, a heart after His, and total surrender, knowing all He does is good.

We see a lot of competition in the church because we are not programmed to see deployment or assignment outside the church. We confine God to religion, forgetting the entire world belongs to Him. We place so much emphasis on sin and judgment, whatever our version of holiness is, being rapture ready (a false concept as it is taught), and on making sure we don't look like the world. We have "separated" ourselves right out of the perfect will of God and God's commission for us to go into all the world and compel them to come. We arrogantly believe that if we stay within the four walls God will somehow drive them in droves to our doorstep. Who is going to come running after a God we never allow them to see? We are supposed to get out there in all facets of the world and let God shine through us.

We have become so religious and pharisaical that we arrogantly assume if there is a call on someone's life, it must be in the confines of religion. We aren't taught that anything else is holy if it has nothing to do with religion. Sure we will affirm a select few careers based on our emotional attachments to them, but let someone say that they are called to Broadway. We have a whole discourse on why that cannot be the will of God if we can't readily identify how souls might be saved. God forbid you should have a call on your life that will eventually end your season of church membership. You're definitely not hearing from God. It's no wonder everyone is internally battling for a place to fit in. If the emphasis of worship is placed on faithfulness to church, reading your bible, serving in the church, and giving alone, so many will never deploy.

The world has changed drastically since the bible days. There's so much more to compete with to get the world's attention. So what does God do? He infiltrates! Through you and I!

What concerns me is that we serve a God that we are afraid to explore. We have locked Him into very specific and fine line characteristics that cause us to overlook how big, vast, and wide He is.

I remember Tasha Cobbs, a well-known gospel singer recorded a song with a well-known rapper Nikki Minaj. I can neither confirm nor deny any instruction from God, but I remember the "saints" having a fit. I get it. To the sanctified and dedicated to religious holiness, Nikki was quite scathing. She wouldn't have been many people's choice for a gospel duo. Tasha is called to the mountain of entertainment. I expect her through God to have influence on it with all others on that mountain, and to deploy in whatever way God instructs.

People were ready to suggest that Tasha lost her way without any consideration for Nikki. Since Nikki didn't readily change her life, get baptized, renounce her career, and get ordained, we assumed there was no God in it. The God I have encountered makes Himself available to the Nikki's of the world, and the Nikki's of the world need to know that.

Nikki was bashed because the people didn't see immediate change after she did the song, but we will never know what the seed that was planted is intended to produce. We expect anybody that a Christian hangs out with in Hollywood to come to God *now* or separate from us, yet we will tarry and ask the church for years to pray that our children get saved. If our unsaved child is caught singing a hint of a gospel song or doing anything related to God, we will shout all through the house and testify that God is working on them even when nothing about their lifestyle changes. We are just glad to see a hint of Godly influence (I am a parent, I know), why wouldn't we keep that same energy for anyone else? I have seen devil worshippers come to Christ after years of possession. God can do all that but Hollywood is off limits?

I am placing a lot of emphasis here because God wants to gather His people into citizenship from everywhere. He is not going to entrance them and "mummy lead" them to your Tuesday night Bible study. He told us to go get them! We must be open to where they are and how God chooses to gather them. We must shift and make it safe to explore God. We must not assume that the presence deploys us all the same. We must not assume that what brings God glory is confined to our perception. His ways and thoughts are higher. We love to quote that, but we won't always allow it to apply.

I did not at the time of writing this book see Nikki come to God. I also didn't see Tasha renounce her calling and her God to start stripping. She is still in position deploying. Whatever God wanted from that, if anything, is up to Him. The point here is not Nikki or Tasha, it's about understanding that

God said His word would go out and accomplish what He wants and it will prosper where He sends it. He didn't say it depended on opinion or location. We need to know we too are a Word, we need to know the written Word, and we need to know the God we serve in new and exciting ways without discarding the old. There is so much more we are not tapping into.

I don't care if a person is adamant that they worship the devil and you will not sway them, if we knew how to live in the presence of God and deploy our authority from that place we could bring that spirit completely under subjection. Jesus just arrived in the area and demons started begging Him to leave. We have that same access and opportunity because we are too prideful to acknowledge our own spiritual shortcomings; we decide that we must just shake the dust! We don't "shake the dust" and write people off based on *our* weaknesses, inabilities, and lack of power or authority. When we open wide ourselves to Host His presence, we will we sense His heart, not our own. We will suggest that God is not interested in delivering people we have never even asked Him about because we don't live in His presence, and we don't possess His heart. He does not come down to our emotional and opinionated level. He calls us to ascend into His.

I need someone to know right now, from someone called to the mountain of religion, that you are not crazy because you sense or know that what God is calling you to is not the church and is completely unorthodox. God is not boxed in. We spent quite a lot of time marveling in the creative wonder of God, you think He forgot suddenly how to be creative?

You might be a trailblazer on your mountain, or there may be others like you. The more of us that deploy in more areas in the earth, will be the more that others will see we should not box God in.

I want to be very clear, because there are always extremist naysayers who want to try to convince the world that anyone who speaks about God in this way are grace only peddlers and heretics. I believe in holiness. He told us to be holy as He is holy. Every instruction you get must come from Him. I've said over and over again we must learn to live in His presence. God will never deploy us into sin. He is not telling us to go strip to reach the strippers or to practice snorting cocaine to reach the drug addicts. He will never altar His reputation in that way, but He might tell you to go to the clubs and bars and draw them. He might point you toward a motorcycle club to be an influence. He might send you into a crack house or to a prostitute. He might place you in entertainment including sports to be a light. He might give you a job that allows you access to inmates and use you to deliver them. He might tell you to go get the list of inmates and write them letters just to encourage them. He might give you credibility with gang bangers and drug dealers. He might use you as a songwriter and producer with influence over more than just gospel artists. He might call you to law enforcement.

We will continue in this thought next section, but I really want you to get in your soul that you serve a God of infinite possibility who wants complete control and trust no matter what people say. I remember when praise dance was forbidden, now it's an entire ministry included in the office of psalmist (also a prophetic office). You and I cannot wait for people to change their hearts and minds to deploy. They are not our masters. **God** is our Sovereign. He knows whom He is trying to reach and how He wants to accomplish His will.

We will never be as influential in the earth as God has required of us taking sips of Him through the straw we allow Him room to occupy. We must open ourselves wide to Him -- so completely to Him that He can display the infinite possibility of whom He is through us. We must cease to be so "avoid hell" focused that we forget our duty to His presence and carrying Him into the earth. Religion has taught us to be hoarders; to collect enough God to assure our seat in heaven, but God is an expansive King with an expansive kingdom that He wants displayed in the entire world. He is not yours to direct or contain for self-maintenance. I'll say it like we tell our children: learn how to share!

Let's look at the concept of the "mountains" which should open our minds to the many ways we can be deployed.

The Seven Mountains – He Deploys us everywhere

In 1975, Bill Bright, founder of Campus Crusade and Loren Cunningham, founder of Youth With a Mission (YWAM), developed a God-given, world-changing strategy. Their mandate: Bring Godly change to a nation by reaching its seven spheres, or mountains, of societal influence.
They concluded that in order to truly transform any nation with the Gospel of Jesus Christ, these seven facets of society must be reached: Religion, Family, Education, Government, Media, Arts & Entertainment and Business.

Let me say that this is a language that you will not find in your Bible, but before you write it off as irrelevant, I want you to study this because while the language "7 mountains" is not found in the Bible, its revelations can be researched and backed up in the in the Bible. As I have taken the time to study this and pray about it, I have received the permission to share. Remember, pleading the blood is not biblically backed either, but we do it, and God does respond to our intent.

As we study these mountains, this is intent to help us understand the broader scope of Satan's rule, and our responsibility to follow our purpose, which will undoubtedly land us on one of these mountains to "shine" (live our purpose and expose others to God and Kingdom citizenship)

As an example, one of the mountains mentioned is the mountain of marriage and family. While we do not find the language "the mountain of marriage and family" in the Bible, we can search the Bible to see if there is evidence of Satan's attack against marriage and family, and we find that there is as we consider Adam and Eve, David and Bathsheba, the rape of Dinah, and the list goes on.

Another we may pull out is the mountain of Entertainment. We can see through closer observation that in entertainment, Satan is having a field day with his sexually perverted agenda, anti-God agenda and the same is true for media. With some search of the Word we find these same perversions mentioned throughout the Word. The language is indeed creative, but the revelations therein are real, and again, are biblically backed.

The mountains I will list below, and I want you to spend some time seeking God about who you are and why you are here specifically. Make that your prayer. As God begins to answer you (and He will answer you in His way), take notes, then come back and review these categories to see where you might fit in. You may find that you have a primary one as I do (religion), and that you may have some authority and influence on others as well. Don't let tradition cause you to shut down or dismiss any part of what you are sensing in you. I came form a denomination that didn't initially ordain women as anything other than evangelists and missionaries. We most certainly didn't have apostles or prophets, even though they were clearly biblical, including the illustration of women in these roles. Climb up into God and explore with Him. Think outside of the box with Him.

1. Religion

Every society has some type of belief in a superior being or beings. In the east, religions tend to be polytheistic (many gods) or outright idolatrous (such as Hinduism and Buddhism). Although these religions are thousands of years old, they nonetheless continue to thrive today. In the west, Christianity and Catholicism are predominant, but postmodern views are increasingly being accepted and the concept of God is being rejected. This is especially true in Europe.

The Christian Church is described in the Greek language as the ecclesia. Literally translated, the word ecclesia means "governing body." Although we don't condone theocracies, this translation suggests that the Church (or Kingdom) should have great influence in all other spheres that make up a society. With a plethora of categorized religions around the world, it's the Church's responsibility to reach the lost with the love and Gospel of Jesus Christ, and expand the Kingdom in ministerial efforts, both nationally and internationally.

2. Family

In any functional society, the family is the "building block" of the community. Throughout the Bible, you will find familial examples that portray how we ought to live our lives today. God desires that men, women, and children within a family be united as one in His love. After all, He is the ultimate Father (Romans 8:14-17).

Families all over the world have been under constant and prolonged attack. Today, the assailants are fatherlessness, divorce (50% rate in secular and Christian marriages), abuse, sexual perversion, pornography, and other negative influences have brought great dysfunction to life. God is calling fathers and mothers (both spiritual and biological) to bring order to the chaos that the enemy has unleashed against families in America. He also wants to bring healing to marriages and relationships within families in order to maintain a moral foundation for children in the future to stand upon.

3. Education

At one time the education system of America unapologetically incorporated the Bible, prayer to the God of the Bible, and biblical values in every aspect of school life. Not coincidentally, this system produced a people that produced the most powerful and prosperous nation the earth has ever seen.

Now, the children of our nation are inundated with liberal ideologies, atheistic teaching and postmodern principles in our public schools and in most universities (including many Christian institutions). Put simply; they are being indoctrinated with often false, biased and anti-biblical information.

A re-introduction of biblical truth and Bible-centric values is the key to renewal and restoration in America's and the world's failing educational system.

4. Government

Proverbs 14:34 states that, "righteousness exalts a nation, but sin is a reproach to any people." Many times, as exemplified in the Old Testament, a nation's moral standards are dependent on those exhibited by its leaders (or predominant political party). While each individual is responsible for his or her own sins, the fact remains that people are greatly influenced by those moral (or lack thereof) that popular leaders adopt.

The progressive liberal agenda and the extreme right agenda empowered by well-known men and women have made significant gains in the political arena over the past few decades. We must see a shift in this arena in order to preserve the Christian heritage and Kingdom citizenship God intended. The goal is to put in place righteous political leaders that will positively affect all aspects of government. It is possible!

5. Media

The media mountain includes news sources such as radio, TV news stations, newspapers, Internet news and opinion (blog) sites and etc. The media has the potential to sway popular opinion on current issues based upon its reporting, which is not always truthful or accurate. To bring transformation to the mountain of media, Christians who are gifted for and called into this type of work must be willing to report righteously and truthfully in the secular marketplace.

6. Arts and Entertainment

On this mountain we find some of the most influential forces shaping our society. Music, filmmaking, television, social media, and the performing arts drive the cultural tastes, values and standards of a nation's citizens, particularly its youth.

With a heavy reliance on the strong appeal of sex, drugs and alcohol, the arts and entertainment industries wield significant influence. The body of Christ needs powerful, righteous men and women who are not afraid to take their God-given talent into the arts and entertainment arenas. People ready to further His purposes, while impacting those who are lost in darkness and would not otherwise be interested in any kind of Christian message in traditional forms.

7. Business

The ability to literally create wealth through ingenuity, enterprise, creativity and effort and is a God-given gift and a universal impulse. The markets and economic systems that emerge whenever people are free to pursue buying and selling become the lifeblood of a nation. This includes anything from farms to small businesses to large corporations.

Of course this realm is prone to corruption through idolatry, greed and covetousness. In response, the Church (Kingdom Citizens) must embrace the responsibility to train up those who are called into the marketplace to manage businesses and provide leadership with integrity and honesty. We believe it is the Lord's will to make his people prosperous and that He desires for us to use its wealth to finance the work of Kingdom expansion without our personal lives not left out of that equation. Simply put: Prosperity with a purpose beyond us.

This is War, but don't glorify it.

I want to leave you with these next few thoughts, before we arrive at a workable definition of authentic worship in the next chapter.

As previously stated, I have been blessed to worship and deploy on other continents as well as my own. I have been absolutely in awe of God and almost as equally as disturbed by the obsession with the gift more than the Giver, or the power and authority more than the Source.

I remember deploying in ministry to a church where demonic activity was quite high. The territorial demon as I could see him was an old ancient one obsessed with bondage.

As we drove into the city, I remember sensing an overwhelming sense of gloom, and when we arrived at the facility that spirit had most definitely infiltrated it. This territorial demon had the church in a strong hold. It is difficult to articulate, but the church itself was bound to it, and it was deceptive because it presented as an old ancient man dressed in white, extremely tall, with a long white beard. I've seen some dark spirits and usually they are revealed to me as dark with sinister eyes. This was the first time that I had seen a spirit try to pass off as angelic and wise. I knew it was evil because as it noticed me noticing it, the look of anger that washed over its face was that of a spooked but bitter revival that wanted to know what I was doing there. It wanted me to know that I wasn't welcome, and I got the message. I can't say that I was scared, but I was definitely on guard. He had the church tied and bound to him like a toddler holds tightly to his toy yelling, "Mine!"

I sat in the back office to pray knowing that this was about to get really interesting. I had never experienced anything like this before, so this was one heck of an initiation into operating in this kind of authority. I decided it would be best for me to stay in the back and seek until closer to time to minister, but I honestly couldn't think of what to say other than "Lord don't let there be any demonic manifestations." Clearly I was a novice. I caught myself though. We didn't come to leave demons in position. We came to cast them out. This was not the time to overlook them and do religious business as usual. I shifted into my holy language to manage any fear that was trying to well up in me, and reached up into His presence for authority and anointing (well before I understood the glory and how it works).

Ministering proved to be strenuous. Unlike other places I had been where the people came with expectancy, this place had all the joy and excitement of a graveyard. Looking out at the faces, almost everyone looked like zombies who had no clue where they were or why they were there. I had to reach deeper into the presence and pull harder on my authority. I knew He wanted me to charge the atmosphere so I had to plow and plow to get to the breakthrough I knew God wanted.

The word began to do its work and I could see people starting to come alive. It was go all in at that point. The more they started to look alive, was the more I pulled on the presence of God to work through me by forgetting what was in front of me and opening myself up more to the eternity inside of me. I was outwardly preaching but inwardly climbing into Him to hear.

When it came time for the altar call, so much had been exposed through the word. God took authority over the atmosphere through me, and with Him we began to call out things and cast them out. We prophesied and plowed some more until the power of God hit the majority of us. I was almost shocked that so many who had looked like the walking dead were crying out to get free. Those that remained in the audience were evil spirits growling at me, but I refused to give in to fear.

My friend who was serving as my armor bearer at the time was right by my side and ready. The people were coming through the line and God would prophesy, cast out, speak to, warn, or restore. It felt like the never-ending line straight from hell sent to wear me completely out. The closer we got to the end of the line, the stronger demons began to manifest. At the time I was really tiny, about a size 2. They were falling into me to try to charge me to the floor, but I would escape with a swivel or pivot. Another threw her arms around my waist so tightly that she was crushing my rib cage. With supernatural power I pried her from around me and cast the demon out of her. Others in the line ran screaming from me and out of the building, but then there came this *one*. God spoke right to the bondage in her and that demon went completely off on me. She began to curse me and threaten to kill my youngest son who was with me if I dared deliver this girl.

The leader jumped in front me I thought to deal with it. I was actually grateful at first. If you have ever operated in deliverance ministry, then you know that it can take a lot of you. I had wrestled them off, cast them out, swirled to miss punches and lunges at me, I cannot lie, I was starting to tire.

To my surprise, he didn't step up to help! He stepped up like a kid in a candy store repeating over and over again, "Ooh mommy I want that one." My armor bearer and I stepped back and then closer to each other confused.

He reached in his jacket for his handkerchief and started waving it in her face. He told her to be quiet, but everything in me knew that he wasn't speaking from a place of authority but familiarity. It was "show time" in the middle of my revival! At this point, I am climbing as high up into God as I can to hear because I am in total shock, but I felt God calm me and advise me to watch and listen.

He began to taunt the demon as if to demonstrate that he had it all under control. Then in the next breath he started interviewing it! He couldn't get it to say its name but he could get it to tell me why it hated me so much and what it wanted to do to me because I deliver people and set them free. I was furious. He looked back at me with a smirk as if I was supposed to be impressed by being "affirmed" by a demon. I couldn't for the life of me understand why you would interview and not cast it out, but God began to tell me that these people were not free because he didn't want them to be. He was in his own way in partnership with the demon that had the church bound, and he liked when demons performed because it was a chance to demonstrate how "powerful" he was by the way they reacted to him.

He twirled this girl, he tormented this girl, he used her for his disgusting display, but God let me know that her He would deliver and Him He would repay. As he played with her, others started acting out and I began to pray. I stepped up higher into authority and just let out my intercession. Whatever God wanted said was said and I stepped up to the young lady and cast the demon out of her. There were a few more that God dealt with before He spoke the public rebuke. After all of that, I knew that God wanted more for this man, but he was too obsessed with glorifying power and demons. It broke my heart to know that I would have to leave these people in His care, but God promised me that those He delivered would stay delivered and all I could do was obey His will.

The second night was different. You could see such a change on many of the faces. They wanted more of God and even brought their friends. I ministered the Word then ministered to all those that God told me to. This time as I went in the building, I went in with a higher sense of my authority and a greater confidence. I knew the enemy would test me, but God stepped up in me and shut so much down before it could be disruptive. Some growled in their seats but they dared not move. Others we simply shut down their screaming by commanding silence. Those that slithered we cast out, and God answered my prayer that night to subdue the leadership so that He could have His way.

I knew it was angering him, but he had to be shut down in the spirit. This was not going to be another night of performance and disruption, not on my watch. He invited me in, and I was going to do my job. God wanted these people to know they could be fully free. This man kept them dependent on him under false pretenses to feed his own lusts for power and recognition.

Several of those that God ministered to reached out to me via social media privately to share their horror stories and how they had never felt so free. Several thought it best to leave and several stayed. About three weeks later, another prophet friend of mine was invited to minister there, and I told him, he just wants to use you to prophesy and disturb the demons so he can play with them. I implored him to seek God and be sure this was God. He said God wanted him to go, so as his closest friend at the time, I prayed to see if God would allow me to travel back there with him. I just wanted to cover him because I knew what he was up against. We came separately, but he advised me later he saw that same territorial demon I had seen laughing but angry that he was there.

It saddened me to sit there and see the church back in the same state it had been in, and this time worse. I covered my friend, but God did not give me clearance to intervene. I watched the same thing unfold with the leader evoking spirits to perform while my friend worked the altar and prophesied.

To date, much of the church has cleared out. I believe that he had gotten really sick at one point, and I remember praying for God to completely deliver him.

I wanted to share that story with you, not to glorify myself (or my friend), but to give you an illustration of how a lust for appearance and power can ruin lives and anger God. God sent me there as a rescue for those he knew would get delivered and stay delivered, wake up, and leave. He sent my friend back there to rescue a few others, and after that I'm told membership began to dwindle quickly.

Every gift that God gives is for His purpose alone. This man is not the only one I've seen fall into this state. I have seen others fall so deeply into their lust for power and into their own points to prove about who they are that they have literally manufactured moments to deceive the people.

I will be the first to admit that when I first tasted of God prophesying through me, and when I travelled overseas and watched God extend Himself in me, I was on a high. I was so amazed at God, but I remember Him warning me not to become boastful and to remember whom it is I serve lest I become a slave to sin. When I experienced the story I shared above, it was after that trip. In fact, I got back home, had a week off, and then travelled there to do that revival. I would never do that again today, but I am glad I got to see that only because it humbled me and reminded me that we are not our own. People's lives are genuinely at stake, and there is never a time to play.

I've seen prophets move into divination and con people out of thousands of dollars, I've seen pastors try to work spells on members to control them, and I even had one try to work something on me, but God blocked it and shut him down.

Our identity is in Christ. We have nothing to prove outside of that. We cannot become so enamored with the gifts and deployments, the flattery, and the praise that we defile them. Any of us can fall into the trap of pride as the fame starts attaching to our name, and we can quickly start to become entitled and manipulative. I cannot stress enough to you that you must practice staying in the presence of God. We see way too many scandals and people brought low, because they became apathetic to the presence of God. Once they achieved a certain level of notoriety they forgot God and followed man's elevation. That is the recipe for disaster and being completely leveled.

Ascend into God and let Him elevate you in your due season. He promises to do so. He will never send you where your character can't keep you. We see so many personalities on display instead of God, because people are trying to be affirmed through a platform to make up for their own deficiencies, voids, insecurities, and lack of control in other areas of their lives.

Deployment is not a place for us to practice and perform. A lot of what we see today is man's agenda. I did not understand why God kept pressing me to write the book, but it was the tool he used to heal, break, reset, and restore me *before* He released me. His way is soft and solid not fast and fragile. Everybody wants to be powerful and feel validated, but few want the pressure of the process and refiners fire.

Your gifts should not become your idols, and they are not what validate you. Our role is to glorify and exalt God, not ourselves. In the process God deals with those places of rejection and abandonment, and anything else that could stand in the way of your complete yielding to Him.

His deployments are not weapons either. We don't wield our gifts to manipulate and attack people any more than we use them to glorify ourselves. We don't lord our deployments over others or use them in competition. This is why we must climb up into God and not get caught up in being deployed by man. God's way ensures your stability, man's way assures your downfall.

There is a way, which seemeth right unto a man, but the end thereof are the ways of death. Proverbs 14:12 KJV

Keep your worship pointed toward God, not on your gifts.

Chapter Reflections

1. All of us battle some form of pride that stems from a place in our history that affects us emotionally. What are some areas in your life that need to be addressed so that your deployment does not become a platform for compensating.

2. Can you identify things that God asked you to do that you have not yet done?

3. How has this knowledge about battle strategies changed your perspective of how you see your assignments?

4. What did you learn about the dangers of glorifying your gifts and deployments?

5. Is there a mountain you feel God is drawing you to? Which one? Why?

6. What assignments have you put off that you perceived were not that urgent? Now that you understand assignments as battle strategies, in what ways can those assignments impact kingdom and destroy Satan's agenda

7. Are there any ways that religion has stifled purpose for you that you can identify?

Part 3
Redefining Worship: Seeking & Relationship

Exploring worship through relationship. Tell me how to become the deployment God intended.

CHAPTER SEVEN

So after all that, what is Authentic Worship?

"

God is a Spirit: and they that worship him must worship him in spirit and in truth. John 4:24 KJV

Authentic worship is not adoration alone. It is not contained in a service, nor expressed in religious piety and adherence to rules. Worship is not an experience. Worship is a lifestyle, a lifestyle that is one of supernatural expectation. Before we categorize it, let's tie in all we have learned thus far.

❖ God had an original man for man to dwell in His presence and reproduce Him in the earth through pro-creation, so that human kind would mirror the glory of heaven. Man was to guard it and cultivate worship in the earth, but it had to be man's choice.

❖ Satan's deception caused man to fall causing sin to enter the earth, and thereby robbing humankind of dominion, presence, identity, authority, and eternal life.

❖ Jesus – God in the person of Jesus, His son, enters in *human form* from eternity into time to restore humankind back to the presence of God and kingdom citizenship, and to take authority over death by sacrifice and resurrection, so the possibility of eternal life would be made available to us again.

❖ Jesus in human form, models for us what living in the presence looks like and what authority and access we have by simply being completely surrendered to God. That surrendering allowed Him complete jurisdiction and authority to exercise (in Satan's kingdom) the will of God wherever it was to be expressed from water into wine to countless forms of physical healing, compassion for sinners, and teaching us not to be deceived by this life. There is one that has always been God's plan, and we must get back to it.

❖ Before His ascension, Jesus passed into humanity (from eternity into time), the kingdom keys (which we explored as all the authority of Heaven to execute the will of God on earth) and the Holy Spirit to be a lingering presence with us as our Guide.

Our job today is to continue in the work of Jesus to be kingdom ambassadors for God in the earth, by **living** in the presence of God, taking on our new identity, embracing our authority, and executing (deploying) the will of God at His every command.

We said earlier He desires to be known. He is a glorious King with an expansive Kingdom He wants made available in every part of the earth before the earth is no more as we know it. There is so much deception down here that we must be awakened to, that He deploys us in all types of ways everywhere. We said earlier that we must be completely open to *however* He chooses to use us (deploy us) at any given moment. So what is authentic worship?

Worship is a Revelation

Most of us praise the God we hear about, read about, sing about, and preach about, but there is a difference in knowing about someone and living intimately connected with them. Knowing about God has forged in us a great level of respect, and visitations we have felt have driven us into emotional response, but none of that is intimacy. It's wonderful, and it is necessary, because He inhabits the praises of His people. He visits to receive it, but even as powerful as many experiences have been, we tend to leave Him in that moment and live from experience to experience.

You cannot claim intimacy with someone until you really know them up close and personal. God designed humankind to live in His presence. When man fell, we lost that luxury. To be restored to that intimate place, you must have a revelation of who He is. Many of us believe that we do know Him, but if that were true, we would be couriers of His presence and not just temporary stewards of His anointing.

Revelation requires an encounter. Let's revisit Peter. Peter and the other disciples travelled with Jesus and watched all the wonderful things He did. A few ascended with Jesus up the mountain and witnessed His transfiguration. God, who had been a distant idea, and an object of affection and reverent penitence, was now present among them in His Son, and they could not seem to grasp the reality of what was right in front of them.

Knowing the time was soon approaching for crucifixion, Jesus asks His disciples who do men say He is. They rattle of the many ideas and Jesus interrupts the responses to ask who do *they* believe He is. Peter emphatically states, "Thou art the Christ, the Son of the Living God." To which Jesus praises Peter and tells him that revelation came to him from God, and because of His revelation, he would be mightily used to spread this revelation.

What was so powerful about what Peter said, that caused Jesus instantly to affirm him? Peter wasn't giving Jesus adoration nor was he still unsure of whom Jesus was. When he spoke, he stepped out of his present reality and into his permanent authority and identity. He stopped seeing Jesus as man and understood that he was literally in the presence of God. The presence is not a place of speculation. It's a place of revelation, and you will never leave speculation without one. In fact, like Peter, when you consciously enter it, you will be affirmed in your identity, drenched in your authority, and deployed accordingly. Having a revelation of God is also having a revelation of who you are—not as you define you, but as He sees you. It is there that you will connect with the Word out of His mouth that you are. Everything shifts from that place.

That kind of opening up to Him is a collision with Him as Eternity invading time. This is not about a prophet speaking over you or you having some inkling about your calling. No. This is about understanding that the collision that just happened between you and God made Him your dwelling place, and everything that you do will be done from that place, which means the glory—the very presence of God Himself has entered the atmosphere and the supernatural must occur.

Worship is living in the Presence.

Why is this so important? Aside from what we just mentioned, in a true encounter, like Jesus, we learn to do nothing apart from Him and can always sense Him. So many of us claim to know Him but have so much trouble sensing Him. It is not possible to dwell in the presence of God and have no clue of what His will is at any given time. He is power. He is authority. He is answer, He is will. He is miracle. He is revelation. He is *all*. We have so many questions that would be answered if we would just make it our lifestyle to house Him. Jesus didn't do anything randomly. He came up on a situation and knew instantly what the Father wanted deployed. Because He was a host for God, the presence of God in Him and through Him did all the work.

We assume we need some special endowment and fancy words to see these awesome wonder occur. You don't. You just need to house Him and the supernatural will occur.

Worship is carrying the Glory.

Most of us ask to be anointed. There is nothing sinful about that. It is the anointing that destroys the yoke, and we can be temporarily endowed to accomplish something for God, but it is just that, temporary. The application of the **anointing** takes the indwelling, infilling and outward overflow of the Spirit upon the believer to execute the will of God in that moment.

The glory is not the anointing. The glory is where our sights should be set when we consider what authentic worship really is. The **glory** requires the believer to ascend into the life of **God** to bring down the literal living presence of God from eternity into NOW. We often say that the glory was in the place, but if the literal manifest presence of God did not enter so that the absolutely supernatural could occur, that was not the glory.

When we have an encounter with God, we are retained there in His presence. The reason we must be glory carriers, is so that others may see the eternal God in us and have the same encounter that we had, that will cause them to House God too. You can't unsee a transfiguration. You can't forget a supernatural encounter. You can't forget the feeling of knowing you just encountered the undeniable presence of God. We don't live for glimpses of God. We live to pursue and carry into the earth the person of God. The more we live in His presence is the more He can fill us with His personhood. The more we are filled with Him is the more we can give of Him in the earth. The more we give Him to the earth, is the more the kingdom is expanded, Satan is defeated, and new recruits deploy!

Worship is Obedience

When we think of obedience, we tend to break that concept down into obeying God and obeying His Word. That's actually accurate, but the focus tends to be solely on abstention from sin and the inevitable consequences. So we look for the rules to follow instead of searching out the Sovereign. Without revelation, there is no advancement. The Word is full of plain sight expression of who God is and who you are, but you need the revelation to see it. The Holy Spirit's job is to guide you to it, and in so many ways He does. You know that feeling you keep getting to give God more of your time? Yes, that's meant to lead you higher than you have ever imagined.

We state often that obedience is better than sacrifice. That's the truth! God was communicating to a bunch of apostate citizens. We defined apostasy earlier as defecting back to living under Satan's rule instead of God's by choice. God was their God in name only. He was not the God of their hearts. It was evident in their idol worship. They assumed that because they were the promised people, God was not going to abandon them. They were misusing the word He sent through their generations to excuse their apostasy. They lived under the rule of Satan devotedly, but continued to make their ritual sacrifices. God was letting them know they could keep their meaningless sacrifices, it was their complete surrender to Him that He was interested in. If the sacrifices weren't being given from a place of sincere devotion, they were meaningless and therefore rejected by God. Remember God is the only judge of the heart. He knows us through and through and determines what state we are in.

So we learn from this that obedience is complete surrender of ourselves to Him. It doesn't stop at salvation alone. It requires repentance, which we previously defined as stepping out of one life where we are mastered by our humanity under the direct influence of Satan, and into a completely different life that reveals to us our identity, sonship, and authority, to bring down to earth from heaven God's will.

Worship is Deployment

Authentic worship requires that we deploy. There can be no encounter with Him that does not express Him in the earth. Again, that is to pull His presence from Eternity into time or to Host Him versus visit Him. As we explored the life of Jesus, we saw that he operated as a human from the heavenly realms. We distance ourselves from any comparison to Him, and inadvertently reject our own authority and ability to do the exact same things and more (greater). Deployment is stepping into that authority and exercising it wherever, however, and whenever it is needed. We will continue to explore this in the next few chapters as well, but I will stress again, this is not something to be afraid of apathetic to.

Most of us have never considered worship and obedience this way, and so we have not been made aware of what was missing. The anointing seemed to be enough, when in fact it has essentially been Satan's compromise. He will let you pull on a temporary thing and take the losses, before He will let you discover your identity and gain the legal right to shut his forces completely down. We treat that like it is God's job, and so we pray for God to subdue Him. God in His mercy answers, but He gave us the command and authority to do this in every area of life ourselves.

As we learn to live in His presence, deployment becomes so much clearer. We talked about you being a Word from His mouth, as well as a deployment, and as you combine all that we have shared, you know that true deployment means hosting (housing Him) within you, which gives you access to all of Him to release at any given moment. All that is required of you is that you keep showing up to relate to Him, explore Him, talk to Him, and know Him. Everything that happens as a result of your relentless pursuit is then a given. Imagine that! All this identity, power, and authority, and all the treasures of heaven at my disposal, and God only requires that I desire to know Him intimately and give completely over to disciplined seeking. Hallelujah.

Now that we have defined authentic worship, it is important that you understand how to step into that. Most of us want this kind of life, but we have not been taught how to receive it or what to expect to even know if we are praying in the right way or seeking the right thing. Don't feel bad. Satan initiated religion to keep us blinded to kingdom so that we would never move past the temporary into the authority, which would keep us as poor wretched souls always falling short of more. He is a liar!

I too, had to wrestle my way past him to stay in the presence of God, and it all started just by showing up consistently. The more I showed up, the more the Holy Spirit could reveal more to me. I just kept drawing in saying, *"Lord I know there is more. I want to know what I am missing, I want to walk close with you like Moses did."* In my settling into the devotion to get to that place, I stumbled upon the information that Satan had been keeping from me. God used the Word, His presence, and books on the concept of kingdom to redirect my entire life! It wasn't about me just elevating in title, it was about me understanding my identity in Him, the authority I had access to, the possibility of what that could accomplish, and the determination to carry that out (deployment). In the next closing chapters we will explore the concepts of relationship, seeking, relating to God, and why the Word is critical. This should build up your expectancy, so that when you approach the throne from now on, you will have some direction that will lead you toward deployment and His version of Worship. Before we close this chapter, I want to share a powerful experience that I hope will inspire you as it did me.

I told you that all it took to break into an entirely new life, was my persistence in showing up. As I did, the Holy Spirit began to take me from talking to Him, to the Holy Spirit talking through for me through Himself. That may sound a little weird, but I expressed a desire to really understand what I was missing, I could not articulate what that meant because I had no idea what that even encompassed. The Holy Spirit, knowing my heart was finally yielded, spoke to God on my behalf through just my yearning. The Holy Spirit was literally talking for me by putting on my heart (mind) what to pray. The Holy Spirit also enlightened me through the Word about what I was really asking for, and I began to pray the Word. This opened up a world of experiences to me, and it made me excited to show up instead of it being the dutiful chore it once was.

One night, I showed up, and I had gotten in the habit of after my own speaking to God, to ask the Holy Spirit to take over and guide my prayers. I would continue in adoration and tongues, and whatever hit my heart, I carried up before the throne. It didn't take an entrancing. It just hit my consciousness, and I made no assumptions. If it didn't seem related, I didn't care. I let it out, and some of my most intense transformation and healing came out of that. My posture was just to let God go wherever He wanted.

So back to the moment... as the Holy Spirit took over, it didn't pray through me this night. This time, it carried me in the spirit realm to a location that I knew was in Heaven. I saw this bright light and I could barely make out two large feet and the largest throne my human mind could contemplate. I couldn't see all of the feet—more like a toe or two, but I could feel on my left a being that stretched from the earth into the heavens and knew it was a glimpse of the presence of God Himself.

To my right, I saw the presence of Jesus in two forms, the man figure and the Word, and the Holy Spirit was a lingering white cloudlike presence. The three were having some sort of convening, and it was about me! The Holy Spirit allowed me in on a conversation about me in the realms and they were speaking so well of me. All I could do was weep, and believe me I wept for hours and until I could hardly feel my face

I heard Jesus Himself say that they could use me to accomplish so much in the earth, that I was special, and would not fail them. It was one thing to hold that as a wish in my heart, but to hear the three affirm it was a life-changing experience. If that wasn't enough, I told you that I said I wanted to be as close to Him as Moses was. In an instant I saw what appeared to be a gaping hole in the universe, but it was a nostril. God was bringing His face to me! As He did, I remember leaning into the bedpost and crying profusely just because I was near Him, and He said to me, that He was granting my request to walk that closely to Him.

I was such an emotional wreck after that, I had to be consoled by angels. I remember the picture of a pitcher and oil being poured on me, and when I finally came to, I was completely taken. I could hardly move because it was so empowering. Of course the enemy wanted me to believe it was all in my head, but I have held on to that promise and I am living it to the best of my ability. Like you, I have so much further to go in that kind of exploration.

Many life-altering events have tried to keep me from the throne. Opposition will come, but the Holy Spirit is a relentless lover unwilling to give up on you. I come to the throne expecting to consummate (explored in a later chapter), and I leave with something else to birth. When I think I have finally started to master one deployment, He sends the Word there is more.

You break into everything I have written in this book, by simply refusing to not show up, and showing up expecting so much more of Him than what you know.

Chapter Reflections:

1. In your own way, summarize the definition of authentic worship. Make it personal.

2. What hits your spirit (understanding) most when you consider the authority we all should be exercising as compared to the faith life we have accepted?

3. Journal any enlightenment the Holy Spirit has given you from the information in this chapter.

CHAPTER EIGHT

Relationship Matters!

> "
> *He was in the world, and the world was made through him, yet the world did not know him. He came to his own, and his own people did not receive him. But to all who did receive him, who believed in his name, he gave the right to become children of God, who were born, not of blood nor of the will of the, flesh nor of the will of man, but of God. John 1:10-13 ESV*

We have talked a lot up to this point about relationship being essential to our deployment in a variety of expressions. From Adam to Jesus to us, we know that there is a higher call that we must answer. In the following chapters we will build upon this concept of relationship by exploring critical facets of it. For now, I want to continue to explore with you this notion of **living in the presence** by building up your expectancy. Without knowing what we should be expecting, we cannot know what to reach for. I warn you there will be more repetition, but Father is ensuring that I drill these concepts into you so that you see how it all connects to authentic worship.

Living in the Presence

First, the **Presence of God** is all of God. Remember God is God the Father, God the Word (the Son), and God the Holy Spirit. For this purpose we must see them as one intentionally. Being in the presence is a time of deep intimacy with our Father (all 3 persons as one). It is that place of knowing Him and being fully known by Him. It is in that inner place, that oneness with our Father, that we experience the **Presence of God**. It is there that the mysteries of **God** are revealed. Living in His presence means Eternity (God Himself) is hosted in our being (just as He was with Jesus in human form), and gives us immediate access to unlimited supernatural power and ability, as well as the authority to deploy it. We are accustomed to limited encounters with God through visitations such as through the anointing and even miracles, but living in the presence allows us and the world around us to experience the very presence of God and supernatural life at all times. God desires this for us all.

What Living in the Presence Produces

There is no possible way to express all of Eternity (The Eternal God) in one book or even volumes. Please note, the following is broad stroke explanation. God is infinite, and capturing that in a few paragraphs or a lifetime is virtually impossible. There will always be more to discover about God, and we will spend our lifetime capturing and releasing as much of Him as we can.

Presence produces transformation

Much like Jesus experienced as we discussed His transfiguration, living in the presence also initiates our transfiguration of sorts. In His presence we are transformed from one unconscious state of living under Satan's rule to being made alive through Christ in God with the authority to operate on His behalf. Jesus left that transfiguration and immediately encountered demonic possession. His time in the transfiguration released in Him something that He needed to execute God's judgment in the earth realm. We should not glaze over that. Every single time that we truly encounter God we should be in expectancy for the next release of Himself into us to then deploy in the earth. Living in the presence keeps Him dwelling in us and makes us ready at all times to act on His behalf. Transformation is life-long. The possibilities in Him are endless and are as accessible as you make yourself available to Him.

Presence produces identity

The world will most assuredly try to dictate the path that we should follow in life. Not all of it is sinful, but it does not direct us toward God. You only need to pay attention and you will note that the world offers us its standards and opinions constantly on what is considered acceptable. Its focus is centrally on our perceived weakness. We are psychologically programmed to see ourselves as flawed. We are so flawed that in order to be considered even close to acceptable, we have to be a certain weight, a certain height, a certain level of educated, and the list goes on. We are consistently oppressed by all of the ways that we don't seem to measure up.

The Bible tells us that without a vision, the people perish. That is not a motivational statement to get you to get up and launch something—well not in the sense that we typically express it, but what it reveals to us is much deeper. We said earlier that authentic worship requires that we have a revelation of who He is. We get that by consistently living in the presence.

Living in the presence also pulls us out of the matrix of trying to find and define ourselves through the chaotic notions of this world. The text reveals to us then, that to not have the revelation of God and your identity in Him, leaves life as chaotic and unstable, purposeless and powerless.

The presence reveals to us our **sonship**. Through Christ and our belief and acceptance of Him, we have been adopted as the sons and daughters of God. By that adoption, we receive the justification necessary to live in His presence and all legal rights concerning us are taken from the hands of the enemy and are permanently transferred over to God. We also through sonship have unlimited access to the Eternal God and the supernatural. As we give fully over to God, God reveals to us who He is, and who we are according to His will. There are some parts of this identity that all His children share, such as the ambassadorship God requires of us, and the authority that we are given to legally execute judgment on all demonic illegality. Then there is a will for us as individuals that gives us a primary focus on whatever mountain God wants taken down. When we operate outside of God's true identity for us, the enemy has no legal obligation to release us from His torment. An identity that is not established from the presence of God is established from only one other place—the matrix of Satan's rule. If you are not seeing the power of God truly working in your life to establish your authority, you are most likely void of presence.

Presence produces authority

We have discussed this a great deal already, but as a reminder: authority gives us jurisdiction. That is the legal right to pursue and render judgment on all demonic illegality and activity. This was passed down to us through Jesus as recalled in Luke 9:1-2.

Presence produces influence and repentance

A powerful result of living in the presence of God versus settling for visitations; is that your very existence becomes an influential beacon for everyone around you. Moses went up into the presence of God for 40 days and nights. By the time he came down from the mountain he carried so much residue from the presence that his face shone as bright in the sun, and the people could not help but see the God in Him to the point of their own discomfort.

We are certainly not trying to draw people to God through fear, but you too can live a life so entrenched in Him, that you will attract others to Him in a way that causes their repentance. Repentance here is defined as a complete turn from being ruled over in an illegitimate government under Satan, to a victorious citizenship in God's kingdom that will begin the process for their deployment as well.

The presence will give you authority, access, and influence in places you never imagined. We don't pursue presence solely for this personal glory, but because God wants to be broadly known and experienced, it will put fame on your name.

Presence produces faith, trust, and confidence in God

We cannot release authority if we don't believe it exists. God requires that we ascend higher into Him, because it is in that process that we come to know more about whom He is by the way He deals with us. He may heal us, love on us, correct us, comfort us, etc. As we have these experiences that shift us from fearing His presence to relating to Him (discussed later), we learn about His character and nature. The more of Him we experience increases our faith, confidence, and trust in Him. This is a starting point for much of what we desire in this natural life such as marriage. Everything hinges on our relationship with Him. No prayer, no presence, no power. The consequence of that, being a lonely, stagnant, and defeated life.

Let me add that God loves us so much that He sends us constant reminders about what He wants to do for us. If you are experiencing that, and find yourself quite frustrated by hearing it but not seeing it, it is because He is beckoning you to the throne for how to access it. Even if you aren't necessarily experiencing that, there is always a beckoning. Draw closer to Him.

Finally, the closer we draw to Him gives us the confidence and assurance that we can perform victoriously for Him. That does not mean that we don't experience some nervousness or even fear at times, it just means none of that overrides whom we know He is and that we can trust in what He says.

Presence produces the felt experience of unconditional love

Through the sacrifice of Jesus we know God loves us unconditionally. The presence allows us to build on that bridge of love and experience it in entirely new ways. One key way, is that our perception of worthiness and ourselves is so transformed in His presence that we can allow ourselves to accept his love. We must become completely unraveled and undone in His presence so that He can minister to every aspect of our being. Experiencing His love and expressing that outwardly in your identity goes hand in hand. You can never produce what you don't believe about who you are. This is in part why He requires a closer relationship with Him above and before releasing us to deployment.

Presence produces more of the Holy Spirit in us

The Holy Spirit is the third God-person of the Trinity. He was there at the creation of the world, He is the spirit that anointed Jesus and gave Him His supernatural power and authority, He is the spirit that raised Jesus from the dead, and He is the spirit that makes us alive in Christ. We are commanded to be filled with the Holy Spirit. That is not a one and done, I spoke in tongues and there's my evidence. Remember He is God and infinite. As we live in the presence we are dominated by the Holy Spirit, which helps us to relinquish all control and renders Him free to break our attachments to sin and any legal right the enemy may have to us. Living in the presence allows the Holy Spirit to examine and saturate every area of our lives.

Presence produces deployment

Finally, as we make our home in Him, and completely surrender to Him, He can deploy us in the earth to carry out His will. This should be our ultimate goal next to intimately knowing Him. That is to *be* **all** He wants and not just *know* what He wants.

The only barrier and limitation to your living in the presence of God is you. You determine how much of Him you carry based on how much you show up to receive from Him and the attitude you approach Him with. You either expand or limit your capacity to receive more of Him by either completely opening up to Him or carelessly carrying Him. To not even attempt to become what you have read in all these pages, or to allow the enemy to influence you to put off seeking (relentlessly pursuing) Him, is to carelessly carry Him, and that has dangerous implications. The limitations you put on yourself are also limitations you put on God. Remember, you are a Word from His mouth. To renounce even jokingly any part of His will for you is to label Him a liar.

You have read how essential it is that we carry on the work Jesus started and even what that means to God. We cannot say that we genuinely love Him and remain unconcerned with all that we now know. You've got to make the decision to seek Him with all you've got.

Chapter Reflections

1. How has your life impacted your ability to see yourself as God does?

2. What are the barriers that exist between you and God that would keep you from experiencing what the presence produces?

3. Assess your prayer life. In what ways have you been limiting your ability to get to know Him more than you do?

4. How much time do you honestly make for God and the Word each day? How has that limited your ability to be fully deployable?

5. Outside of any title you hold, and aside from any clues you may have received about your destiny (through the prophetic or an inner knowing), have you received the full revelation of your identity? If so, what is keeping you from deploying as God wants? If not, you are strongly advised to seek Him until you have it.

CHAPTER NINE

What is Seeking Anyway?

> "
>
> Seek the Kingdom of God above all else, and live righteously, and he will give you everything you need.
> Matthew 6:33 NLT

We would be remiss to have all of this wonderful conversation about God's original intent, holy war, power and authority, relationship and presence, and not take the time to evaluate one of the most important scriptures that points us directly to it all. Matthew 6:33 offers to us an exact strategy to follow in order to discover the Kingdom, how to become a citizen, how to live in the presence, and access the authority and our rights as citizens, and how to discover our purpose.

We have revisited the chapters and defined authentic worship. We have discussed why relationship matters and what living in the presence of God produces, and in this chapter, we will break down this text to help you enter into deeper relationship with God in a way that will point you toward your purpose and make you ready for deployment.

Seek Ye:

My biggest challenge was that I didn't really know what seeking was. I assumed that my regular attendance and commitment to church and activities was enough. That of course did not leave out prayer and study of the Word (the Bible), but I will admit here that I was not as committed as I needed to be to Bible study or prayer. My approach to Him was methodical and one of duty. While we are obligated to seeking Him, He wants us yielded and contrite heart, not a press in to try to manipulate the system by activity that produces no power or authority.

There is a story in the Word that inspired me concerning seeking. It is found in Luke 15: 8-10 noted as The Parable of the Lost Coin.

"Or suppose a woman has ten silver coins$^{}$ and loses one. Doesn't she light a lamp, sweep the house and search carefully until she finds it? ^{9} And when she finds it, she calls her friends and neighbors

together and says, 'Rejoice with me; I have found my lost coin.' [10] *In the same way, I tell you, there is rejoicing in the presence of the angels of God over one sinner who repents."*

While the text refers to the way Heaven rejoices when a soul comes into Kingdom citizenship, it ministered something about seeking to me. I found that seeking is a **relentless pursuit** of God. It is a search, in this case a search for God that leads into building a relationship with Him.

The onus was placed on me. This seeking has nothing to do with trivial duties and obligations to church and its functions. Like the coin, it suggests importance, something of value that must be found no matter what it takes. And when it is found—when purpose and presence is found I share it with others. I am a visual person, so this little parable helped me to understand seeking in an entirely new way.

First:

To put something first is to place it above all else. It has a special position in your heart and life. You will do whatever it takes to maintain its position. It is of extreme importance to you. This is where the truth of about our relentless pursuit of God is put to the test. How often have we said God is first but can hardly find time for God throughout our day, or cannot let go of something or an idea we are clinging so desperately to?

God is clear about being first. Anything in God's way of being our first and highest priority, anything in the way of us relentlessly pursuing—chasing after God, Kingdom, and purpose, we must surrender to God or He will snatch it from us.

The Kingdom of Heaven:

We defined kingdom much earlier as "Thy will be done on earth as it is in Heaven."

We discussed that from the inception of the world, there was a plan for it. Before your conception there was a plan for you—God's will on earth as it was already decided about you and your role in the Kingdom as a citizen, royal priesthood, and ambassador before you exited the womb. Your relentless pursuit of God reveals what that plan for you is and exposes you to an entirely new life in God.

All of us will undoubtedly arrive at the place in our life where we will question our life's meaning or what our true purpose for our existence is. As we pursue God, that answer comes. Again, it is what the enemy (Satan) is desperately trying to keep you from. He does not want you to know your identity or deploy.

And His Righteousness:

Dictionaries define *righteousness* as "behavior that is

morally justifiable or right." Such behavior is characterized by accepted standards of morality, justice, virtue, or uprightness. The Bible's standard of human righteousness is God's own perfection in every attribute, every attitude, every behavior, and every word. Thus, God's laws, as given in the Bible, both describe His own character and constitute the plumb line by which He measures human righteousness.

The Greek New Testament word for "righteousness" primarily describes conduct in relation to others, especially with regards to the rights of others in business, in legal matters, and beginning with relationship to God. It is contrasted with wickedness, the conduct of the one whom, out of gross self-centeredness, neither reveres God nor respects man. The Bible describes the righteous person as just or right, holding to God and trusting in Him (Psalm 33:18–22).

True and perfect righteousness is not possible for man to attain on his own; the standard is simply too high. The good news is that true righteousness is possible for mankind, but only through the cleansing of sin by Jesus Christ and the indwelling of the Holy Spirit. We have no ability to achieve righteousness in and of ourselves. But Christians possess the righteousness of Christ, because "God made him who had no sin to be sin for us, so that in him we might become the righteousness of God" (2 Corinthians 5:21). This is an amazing truth. On the cross, Jesus exchanged our sin for His perfect righteousness so that we can one day stand before God and He will see not our sin, but the holy righteousness of the Lord

Jesus.

This means that we are made righteous in the sight of God; that is, that God accepts us as righteous and treats us as righteous on account of what the Lord Jesus has done. He was made sin; we are made righteousness. On the cross, Jesus was treated *as if* He were a sinner, though He was perfectly holy and pure, and we are treated *as if* we were righteous, though we are defiled and <u>depraved</u>. On account of what the Lord Jesus has endured on our behalf, we are treated as if we had entirely fulfilled the Law of God and had never become exposed to its penalty. We have received this precious gift of righteousness from the God of all mercy and grace. To Him be the glory!

So we pursue righteousness by allowing God to continue the purification process in us until we demonstrate His character through ours for those who are exposed to us and are potential Kingdom citizens.

God also ministered to me that another aspect of living the "Righteousness of God," is done through becoming what God originally intended for us to become. I had other things that I thought I wanted to do, but God's plan for me was to be His prophet and travel the world pointing His people to His Kingdom. I made an exchange of my desires for His as I pursued Him and Kingdom above all else. God places His citizens everywhere, not just in the church. We need only yield.

And All These Things:

As often as I heard this text recited, I often assumed that all these things pertained to blessings that I would get. I was not entirely wrong, there was just more to it than I understood.

Earlier we talked about all that Kingdom affords us, I saw this part of the text as simply all the things that I had been praying for in my limited understanding, but as we looked at the life of Jesus, we know that we also have access to everything God has, from His riches to His power and authority!

Additionally, "all these things" includes the equipping that we need in order to carry out God's will. Whatever God requires you to do, and wherever God chooses to place you, as you obey Him you will discover access, revelation, opportunity, and living your destiny or purpose.

Shall Be Added:

Shall indicates an absolute. It is a guarantee. When a "shall" leaves the mouth of God concerning you, you can bet your life that whatever was spoken will absolutely come to pass.

In this text, "shall" refers back to the "all these things." Remember that "all these things" is bigger than your personal requests and is bigger than what your finite mind can conceive, but it also includes some of your wants such as a spouse, children, a house, and other things you may have petitioned

God for.

All things are a resounding "yes" and "amen," which means "it shall be so" or "it is so," or "I agree." In this case, God agrees that your "all these things" shall arrive in your life exactly when they are supposed to without delay! Glory to God!

Unto You:

There is nothing that is for you that you will miss. Sometimes we worry that God is not going to do what He said, or we fear that we may do something to miss out on something God has for us. That is impossible!

There is a theological belief that encourages people to follow the will of God by using a rather fearful tactic of telling them that they can abort the plan of God if they don't yield. That is a gross lie. It suggests that we have more authority than God if we believe that we can somehow mess up enough to cause a word He spoke over us to die.

In Exodus we read about the Hebrews leaving Egypt, making their way to the Promised Land. God promised them that there was the land of Canaan waiting for them—a land flowing with milk and honey (indicating that there was provision and prosperity there).

As we read into the text, we find that because of sin, an entire generation was wiped out before the Hebrews crossed the Jordan to possess the land. We also learn that

Moses, in his disobedience and anger dishonored God and was not able to cross the Jordan with the next generation into the Promised Land. Did both the Hebrews and Moses abort God's promise? Absolutely not!

God's word did not fail! God promised that Moses would lead the Hebrews to the Promised Land and he did. God promised that the Hebrews (or Israelites) would possess this new land, and they did! He never said the original generation would inherit the promise.

We said earlier that God knows those that are for Him and against Him. God knows those that will yield and deploy and those that will not. God sanctified those that were His for a special purpose, and His word will not ever fail. God; however, is merciful and because of his mercy He gives many the chance to convert and obey even when He knows they will not.

If you are carrying any reservation or guilt, release it to God. We come to God and into greater knowledge of God exactly when we are supposed to. We have missed nothing, and we must not believe that lie.

In our minds we express these things as delays, or abortions, but the fact is, our timing is perfect no matter how long our process has taken or how many mistakes we have made. We say these things to express regret, and of course as we look back, we wish we had done better sooner, but that is our reflection and expression not God's.

Whatever is due you will always find you when it is supposed to. God offers it to us knowing exactly when we will actually pay attention to it, but in his mercy still decides not to withhold the information. At some point, we will "catch up" to that word or cross paths with that word and plan for our lives and fully embrace it if we are in fact a being that God knows will ultimately choose Him.

Life circumstances are a steering wheel. Don't beat yourself for the detours. Even in those we learn valuable lessons, and we learned earlier from Romans 8:28 that all things are actually commanded to work for the good of us who love God and are called according to His purpose. You have not and will not miss a thing that was and is designed to be "unto you!"

We have defined seeking and why relationship matters and what the Presence of God produces in your life. You know that you must release your idols. And if we travel further backwards into previous chapters, we are reminded of the life Christ lived and how it is a powerful model for us today in an ongoing holy war. We know now that we are a Word out of God's mouth and were created as a divine intention, and that it is only in the presence of God—learning to live in it that we can deploy and accomplish His will.

We've covered quite a bit, but I don't want to leave you with big ideas alone. In the next chapter, I will break down for you as thoroughly as I can how to engage in a prayer life that gets results and ultimately leads to your true purpose and deployment.

Chapter Reflections

1. Define what seeking is.

2. . What are some barriers to your seeking that you are aware of?

3. Can you identify any potential idols, in your life, or things that you know are idols? What scares you most about surrendering them?

CHAPTER TEN

Dear Reader, Go! Deploy!

"

And then he told them, "Go into all the world and preach the Good News to everyone. Anyone who believes and is baptized will be saved. But anyone who refuses to believe will be condemned. These miraculous signs will accompany those who believe: They will cast out demons in my name, and they will speak in new languages. 1They will be able to handle snakes with safety, and if they drink anything poisonous, it won't hurt them. They will be able to place their hands on the sick, and they will be healed." Mark 16:15-18 NLT

There are a lot of people that want to be deployed, but few who are really committed to the process of development. We know that we need a relationship with God that is truly intimate and what relentless pursuit is by definition, but it all becomes alive as you develop the discipline to pursue.

In an earlier chapter we looked at Hebrews 6:4-6 and discovered that there is no hope for the one that has all the truth and information before them, but still does not yield to God as their God. I want to be clear, saying God is your God is not the same as relentless pursuit of Him. Salvation grants us kingdom citizenship, relentless pursuit qualifies us for deployment.

I come across so many who say that they know they need to be doing more to pursue God, but they cannot seem to find the motivation to do it. After all that you have read, if that is you, I pray that you have come to realize the necessity of drawing closer to God to discover your true identity and deploy. I pray that you are ready now to address your apathy and step into the fullness of who you are.

We have given you in this book some big ideas as we discussed holy war, Jesus, authentic worship and deployment, but you should not think that it is impossible to become what He wants. Satan wants you to feel so threatened by the notion that you can actually do what Jesus did or that you are a divine deployment, but with God all things are possible. God is not asking you to do anything on your own. He is a sure guide.

Your responsibility, now that you've travelled through time and history with me is simply to start living in the presence to cultivate the relationship with God that He wants from you, so that you can discover your identity and deploy.

When I was growing up, I was taught that we should pray, study the Word, fast if we needed to, and that when we pray, we should not jump right in to a bunch of petitions. They told us the way to get God's attention was to start by worshipping Him and *then* make your requests known. The truth is, they weren't wrong. We do need to study the Word and to pray. We should offer God praise. There is so much power in that.

I did all that. I didn't always do it as consistently as I should have, and I have come across many who have difficulty maintaining the discipline as well. We are not going to go any farther than where we are without prayer and the Word, so we've got to look at a new way to approach both to ensure that we are actually developing intimacy with Him. Otherwise, we will continue to be frustrated by the lack of results, we will become impatient and apathetic, and we will not be able to deploy, which is exactly what Satan wants.

Consider Your Approach. Who Are You Talking To?

Let's be honest. How many times have you jumped in the bed, got nice and comfortable, found that sweet spot, closed your eyes, and then thought, "Aww man, I forgot to pray." You toss a little, you contemplate just doing it tomorrow, or you reluctantly throw off the blankets, sit up begrudgingly, slowly get into posture, and start to try to gear yourself up to pray like revving a car that just won't seem to start.

In some form or another, a lot of us have been in that place where we aren't exactly joyous about developing the discipline. We grunt, we grown, and we get it done because we feel obligated. Or, we simply just ignore the pull. That my friends, is apathy, and Satan does everything He can to make you feel it. You can be absolutely energetic until it is time to crack open that Word.

It's our responsibility to examine ourselves and why we are so averse to doing what we know is necessary. Maybe we are being lazy, maybe we don't feel like we should come to Him because our heart is not right, maybe we don't see the point of it all. Whatever it is, it's got to be your priority to deal with it and to break it, and the only way to do both is to do the opposite of what you've been doing and throw yourself all in.

When I was on the dating scene, I was very adamant (as much as I could be) about how I was treated. I expected respect and communication. Whenever I felt someone's interest waning toward me, or perceived their apathetic nature around spending time with me, or if it became clear they weren't that interested or wanted only what they could get out of me, it was a wrap. Who wants to date someone that never calls them back, half-heartedly responds to texts and emails, acts like it's a chore to spend time with them, and only gets excited to see them when they can get whatever it is they want from them? Whenever I found myself chasing someone down to pay attention to me, I had to catch myself and tell myself, "Girl let it go. He is just not that into you." Sadly, as we do everything we can to avoid the discipline of intimate time with God, we are communicating all the while that we are just not that into Him.

Listen, this is God. This is the Eternal Sovereign who holds the fabric of our very existence in His righteous right hand. He has been our source of comfort. He has made ways that only He could have. He has shown us favor when we did not deserve it, and even when we act a complete fool, He loves us enough to grant us a clean slate everyday. If anybody is demonstratively committed to the cause of "us," it is surely God. He knows us better than we know ourselves, and treats us better than we treat ourselves.

For many reasons, we have seen God as distant, and we have had God presented to us as a mighty ruler with an iron fist waiting to judge us for every little thing we say or do wrong. The over emphasis on avoiding hell has left us with a perception of God that He has done nothing to earn. He never earned our fear of Him. We did that to each other and to ourselves by being overly consumed with sin. He has not given us a spirit of fear, but of power, of love, and of self-control. Reverential awe (another form of fear) is one thing, but we should not be scared to approach Him. We can come to Him as we are indeed, but that should be in reverence and humility.

How you entreat God is the difference between a glorious life of victory and abundance, and a chaotic static life in defeat. If you don't want to be treated like you are a chore, you should most certainly not treat Him as such. We covered a great deal on the subject of apathy. Explore it again as often as you need to until you begin to shift and give Him the love, honor, and reverence He deserves. Identify and press past any form of apathy, and watch your life change.

God is a Relational God!

What aids in our excitement for intimate communion with God, is the understanding that God is more relational than we give Him credit for. We know it in theory, but we just can't help the psychological conditioning that He is angry all the time. One conversation about grace will throw half the church into a tailspin. We believe that we receive grace in certain contexts, but outside of that, we must beat ourselves into submission, we are not to relax under any circumstances lest we let our guard down and fall into sin, and we must drill, drill, drill, that hell is hot and it is real. In the name of righteousness and declarations that holiness is still right, we end up living some of the most miserable and condemning lives, lashing out at everybody and everything.

We do not suppose that we should abuse grace here. God forbid. But to ignore it completely is an imbalanced gospel, which is an imbalanced life. Instead of noting the loving kindness of God and God's relentless passion toward us (expressed at Calvary), we always have to throw that judgment disclaimer in there. Friends, we have to learn to bask in the beauty of God's grace, as intensely as we concentrate on His judgment. There are always consequences for anything that we do, but how we present God to others and ourselves determines how we relate to Him. If we live like we are always in some way letting Him down, a form of fear is expressed when we neglect time with Him or feel unworthy to approach Him. This is why over emphasis on judgment to the exclusion of love and grace is dangerous.

When I really started delighting (losing myself) in Him, I found He was so caring, kind and gentle, and absolutely concerned about me. Grace is not a curse word. Learning to live in the liberty of grace does not mean that one does not take righteousness seriously. Slavery and oppression beat us into submission. Slave masters taught us their version of the word that made them superior, and to keep us in line they used the Word as a weapon. That mentality has travelled down through the generations, and we find that we are still using the Word as weapon over many a pulpit. The only way to change our perception of God is to give ourselves permission to relate to Him differently.

A relational God is affected by our prayers

We said earlier that we have no problem petitioning Him. We even readily recite that God invites our petitions: "*Ask me, and I will make the nations your inheritance, the ends of the earth your possession*" (Ps. 2:8). Jesus says, "*My Father will give you whatever you ask in my name*" (Jn. 16:23). A God that is not relatable is a God that is not approachable. If God were an unconcerned God, immune to any feeling for us outside of noting our every sin, why even go to Him in prayer? God is not unaffected by what we say and what we do.

A relational God is suffers with us.

The Apostle Paul describes God's empathetic love this way: *"Praise be to the God and Father of our Lord Jesus Christ, the Father of compassion and the God of all comfort, who comforts us in all our troubles, so that we can comfort those in any trouble with the comfort we ourselves receive from God. For just as we share abundantly in the sufferings of Christ, so also our comfort abounds through Christ"* (2 Cor. 1:3-5).

God Himself is love. He feels deeply and cares intensely. All throughout the Old Testament we encounter a God who is relentless in trying to get us to see the depth of His love for us. He gave His Son as His ultimate expression of His love, so we should not see Him as one who perceives our pain and suffering as trivial. It's actually limiting for me to describe Him as empathetic, because He can absolutely relate. He created us in His image. Everything we feel, He feels. He is a fellow sufferer who understands our suffering. We should never assume there is any part of us He does not care about. He wants us to cast all of our cares on Him. We are never a bother to Him. He longs to hear everything on our hearts, not just our needs.

A relational God can be imitated.

We have had it drilled into us that we are to be like God. If God is not gracious and relational enough to let you come close, how on earth are you supposed to become like Him? We have tried to imitate God through the Word. We read it, then we try in our own power to be it. The problem with that is, if the Word is not actually made alive in you, you have words but no inspiration.

We will admit that loving our enemies poses some challenges. The Word says that we should, so we try to decide our way into love. How has that worked out? The only one that can teach you how to love in that way is the one who is love Himself. He knows you intimately because He created you, and He knows what it will take for you to get an understanding that you will live out.

It's difficult to imagine how we can imitate a non-relational God. Have you ever noticed that the more you are around someone you start sounding and acting like them in a lot of ways? The amount of time you spend with them makes them rub off on you and vice versa. It is the same with God. We can imitate God because He makes Himself available to us and beckons us to draw closer. A God that is not relational, would never allow you to draw that close. God would not give us this command and then distance Himself from us so far that we could not attain it. We tend to see Him as the God in the clouds, but He is omnipresent and will come as close as you will allow.

I want you to start seeing God as more loving and up close and personal. He yearns for you. He longs to spend time with you. Aren't you more drawn to someone that strongly desires you than you are to someone that avoids you? It's exciting to be in their presence because you will be affirmed and empowered. Don't see time in the Word and prayer as a chore. See it as relational—a time of beautiful, inspired, and transforming intimacy.

Change Your Perspective of Prayer

So we know that God is relational, and that as we draw close knowing He wants us there we can become like Him. Prayer is an overflowing fountain of wealth, and I don't mean just financially. If we never move the needle past petition, or prayer being a duty we have to hurry up and be done with, we will miss out on so much. Relational prayer opens up our entire being to God. When we set aside time to spend with Him, we should come expecting a powerful encounter. There is room for petition, yes, but prayer is so much more.

So many are finding themselves constantly buffeted by the devil, and it because they don't know who they are. Consider this, in Luke 10, Jesus gave the disciples the authority to literally tread on the power of the enemy. To tread on something is to step on it. When you step on something you bind it. You suffocate it and cease it's ability to move any further. The disciples were consistent in missing the message from Jesus. They assumed that He was the only one that could execute such miracle working power (casting out demons, healing, etc.), and they mistakenly assumed that when they were given the chance to participate, they were only able to do so as long as He was around. He passed the presence on to them, and all they had to do was receive and believe.

We don't see ourselves as capable of carrying the kind of power and authority God promised, and that is because we are not spending enough time in the presence of God to learn to adjust to that kind of thinking and power to execute.

The approach to prayer is to avail ourselves to learning intimately the one we serve. Satan is terrified of that. When you go into time with the Most High, knowing that you are going to receive important Intel or another powerful release and encounter, everything shifts. There is a direct correlation between the presence of God and your true identity, and there is also a connection between your identity and your authority. Romans 8:15 speaks to the fact that we shall not receive the spirit of bondage again. Instead we have received the spirit of adoption, and we have the right to cry, "Abba Father!" The Holy Spirit has been gifted to us to help us see our sonship. You must know who you are. God knows that if you never figure out who you are, you will never walk in authority.

I want to be clear, authority is not just about healing the sick and raising the dead. You may be daunted by those ideas. That's ok. You'll get there. We have a responsibility to take dominion remember? Jesus in Luke 9 gave the disciples the authority over all the power of the enemy and the power to cure all disease. *Exousia* is the Greek word used for authority here and it means, "the right to act on behalf of another."

You have been given divine right in the earth to act on behalf of God. If you saw a crime in action or someone breaking the law, you could yell, "Stop in the name of the law" or "Freeze, you are under arrest," but if the criminal does not see your badge, he knows that he is under no obligation to listen to you because you have no authority to arrest him or enforce the law.

When we encounter dark forces and uncover the plots of the enemy, we have the legal jurisdiction to act on behalf of God and to enforce the will of God—whatever that is in that moment. What Jesus did everywhere He went, was undo everything that Satan tried. If a person couldn't see, he exercised His authority and corrected the situation.

How many of us have felt so defeated by the enemy? How many of us have been discouraged, battered, broken, and deceived by him and his tricks? Well, what if I told you that no matter how angry he makes you, he has the legal jurisdiction to torment you, to ravage your family, to afflict your body, to mess with your marriage, to torment your mind, and whatever else he feels like, because you're not wearing your badge? Your title is not your badge.

The presence produces your credentials. Remember when Jesus stepped into the territory (Matthew 8:29) and the demons went crazy and began to ask Him why He was there to torment them early? They had legal jurisdiction. They had free reign, and they were many. Jesus showing up was a violent and unfair interruption to their reign. **You** have that same authority to stop demonic forces dead in their tracks. You have the right to pursue and arrest, confiscate, and destroy. You have to believe it, and you have to be certain that Satan is no way comparable or equal to God. He is already defeated.

Knowing your identity has so many implications for your life and everything God wants you to do. Your approach to prayer has to be to draw close to know Him intimately so that you are always aware of Him, and to receive pertinent information about your present and your future. **Your approach** to the throne *this* way will literally rob the devil of his every authority to come against you. He is obligated to bow to you when you carry the presence of God.

Don't Neglect the Word

The Word and prayer go hand in hand. The Word is as much the voice of God as His audible voice. The Word is authority and it is our constitution and bill of rights. The Word is our history, our present, and our future. It is infallible and it contains the mind of God. The Word is Jesus Himself expressed in written and divine form. In the beginning was the Word (Jesus), and the Word was God and the Word was with God. We cannot then neglect any form of God in any of His persons.

Satan would try to deceive you and have you believe it is not that important. Many have said that the written Word should not be trusted because evil hands have manipulated it. While it is true the hands of man have canonized what they chose to form our Bible, God has never ceased to keep the world from any part of Him, and His power has always been on display through it. How? When we embrace any part of the written word by faith, it comes alive. That is because it is Jesus activating that part of Himself in us. When you think about speaking the Word or putting the Word on a thing, you are putting Jesus literally on it

When you are a citizen, you have citizenship rights. Who advocates those rights for you? Jesus! Why? He swears by Himself through it written because He is it wholly. Except you know what those rights are, you can be easily manipulated and conned. The Word is our constitution. The constitution is not only your guideline for what is expected of you as a citizen. It is also your bill of rights and an outline of how you can expect the kingdom and the Sovereign to act on your behalf. Most of us live defeated lives and aren't seeing the Word fully work for us, because we barely pick it up or read it without correct revelation and interpretation. You cannot exercise legal right and authority over Satan if you are not sure that you have the right. When you don't know your kingdom rights, you don't know to demand them. Jesus as the Word in your life is only as active as you allow and believe. Changes how you see the Word doesn't it?

The enemy wants you to believe so many false things about yourself and God, your authority and your identity, but when you have taken the Word (Jesus) into your heart, you can release it (Him) back out into the atmosphere and put everything out of alignment in its place.

I want to reiterate this so you absolutely get it. I told you that Jesus Himself is the Word. What makes the words come off of the pages is the Word Himself present in you. The Bible says, "Thy Word (Jesus Himself), have I hidden in my heart that I might not sin against God (also Jesus). That does not mean that as long as I memorize the scriptures, I will know them well enough to not sin. Who of us has succeeded in that? Sin will find you no matter how much written Word you know. *This* understanding speaks to literally carrying Jesus within our person (remember the three are one, so this is living in the presence).

When Satan cannot detect Jesus-Word in your heart, you are as much of a threat as a gun without bullets. Having the living Word in the person of Jesus is an entirely different stance. When you speak it from *that* place it works with you in exercising authority. It is through the written Word we encounter Him, rediscover Him often, and hold Him with us.

Knowing what part of Him to pull on at any moment is critical. Jesus/God is liberty. Where the presence dwells Satan must flee, because bondage cannot coexist with liberty.

The Word (Jesus Himself) is your constitution in the courts of heaven. When the accuser has come with His bogus charges, his relentless attacks, and his trumped up stories, you can remind him and God of what the constitution (Jesus) promised, and Jesus as the Word and your advocate shall affirm you and perform. We don't even argue with opposing counsel. When Satan speaks you broke, the constitution says that all your needs are met by Abba according to His riches. When Satan says you cannot stand, the constitution says that you can do all things through Christ who strengthens you.

The Word (Jesus Himself) is totally authoritative, and when it is made alive in you, you have right perspective, right alignment, right understanding, and the right to exercise it. This is why Satan works so hard to keep you from it. He knows it is Jesus. As you begin to develop your intimacy with God, don't exclude time in the Word as part of it. You can't really know Jesus without it, and you won't know what part of Him to pull on when you need it. You're not just picking it up or putting it down. You're picking Him up, and putting Him down.

In some of my worst hours, at times of staring death in the face, in my most broken moments, in my most desperate times, the Word was made alive in me, and its authority did not fail. Wherever God sends it out (even through us), it shall (an absolute promise) accomplish what it was sent to, and it shall prosper!

He sends the Word (Himself) to you today to accomplish in you what He always intended. It shall not fail, and it shall prosper in you as you deploy. Receive it. It is your right.

Let's Recap. The Word is a necessity because:

1. We get to know God (God as all 3) – We come to know God's character through the Word. The more we know God is the more we trust God. The more we trust God, the easier it is to obey God. The more we obey God, our faith in God is increased. As our faith increases, we can be used by God to accomplish His will.

2. We discover God's will - The message of eternal salvation is a vital and dominant theme in Scripture, but the Bible reveals much more—including how God would have us live. Through the recorded examples of biblical figures we can learn what pleases God and what does not. His Word also gives direct instruction to believers on how we should act in every circumstance.

God's inspired and inerrant Word was given for many reasons: to teach us, rebuke us, correct us, and instruct us in righteousness; it was also given so that we may be complete and equipped for every good work (2 Timothy 3:16–17). By reading the Bible on a consistent basis, you can find direction for your life and learn how to best serve the Lord who gave His life for you.

3. We get to know God's Word and the promises therein - Reading through the entire Bible provides an opportunity to better understand Scripture's "big picture." At the same time, we must be careful not to read the Bible just for the sake of doing it.

- ✓ Reading cover to cover vs. scripture in isolation on occasion exposes the entire picture and the total will and heart of God. It's about a King and His Kingdom—A love story for the believer.

- ✓ The Bible is our constitution full of not only governing behavior, but also amazing promises that every believer/citizen is entitled to. Through understanding the Word as Jesus, we release the Word as authority and it performs for us and prospers us.

- ✓ The Word is our defense against spiritual attacks. Knowing what it says with accurate interpretation, and having studied and applied it, holding it in our hearts allows for easy recall when the enemy is working against us. We Hold Jesus the Person and learn Him through the written, and deploy Him through the authority we are promised.

✓ The Word is God's voice alive! Have you ever had a thought or a question and a scripture you came across, or a bible plan you just happened to see popped up and answered you? The Word is one of the ways we hear from God (as all 3) in conjunction with our prayer life. Knowing the Word is Jesus Himself means He Himself is initiating a conversation with you to release that part of Himself into your life.

Am I Hearing God's Voice?

It's an honest question and concern. We must be sure that we know the voice of God, and again that is developed as you make your prayer life relational instead of transactional. Most of those that express to me a fear of missing God, often have trouble discerning His voice. The culprit is always the same—a prayer life (if one at all) that does not maintain the approach or the awareness of the need to know Him. As you approach the throne with intent to build a stronger relationship with Him, He will make sure that you become familiar with How He speaks to you and how you sense Him.

God Speaks:

- ✓ Audibly (In a voice we know is not ours)
- ✓ Through Life Lessons and Experiences
- ✓ In Nature
- ✓ In Dreams & Visions
- ✓ Through the Prophets
- ✓ Through Signs and Wonders (miracles)
- ✓ Through His People/Vessels (In every day conversation or also prophetically, and they need not be a prophet)
- ✓ Through every day things (such as commercials or billboards)
- ✓ And of course… through the WORD (including sermons or worship songs)

If you truly want to hear Him and deploy, you must be relentless in your pursuit of Him and open to hearing Him in every way.

Sometimes we are concerned that we may be hearing ourselves and our desires and not God. That's normal, and it is a reflection of the limitations on our relationship and communion with Him. You will grow so close to Him that you will start to sense Him in every way, but as you work your way to that place, be open, as we said above, to hearing Him in ways He knows you will catch. I dream, I see pictures and visions in my time of prayer, I always hear Him in the Word, I hear Him in nature and in numbers. You will discover your ways.

Don't expect always to be taken up out of yourself somewhere. Sometimes God's voice is heard through the Holy Spirit right inside of you. Remember He dwells in you. It will often sound like your own thoughts unless you hear Him audibly. To assess if it's truly God, look for the characteristics of God in it, assess if it leads you toward Him and what you now know (He expects from you as a worshipper) or away from it, and then back it up in the written Word. Satan will never tell you to do anything that will point you back to God. If there is any inkling of anything that could serve as a distraction from your complete purpose, don't ignore it, and don't make excuses for it.

How Will I know if my Prayer Life is Effective?

Fortunately, this is not a complicated venture for us, because it is impossible to come into the presence of God and not be changed. Remember, He is relational, and He wants us to be like Him. As you build that intimacy with Him you will experience the wonders of Him in so many ways:

- ✓ Personal Experience of God's Love
- ✓ Reminder/Revelations of Promises

- ✓ Character Correction
- ✓ Exposure to Issues / Clarity / Healing
- ✓ Personal Transformation
- ✓ Discipleship & Discipline
- ✓ Assignment & Instruction
- ✓ Testing, Wins & Failures
- ✓ Open Doors to Assignment and Destiny
- ✓ Manifestation of Promises

Those are broad categories that encompass so much, but trust me, you will know that you have been in the presence of God, because every encounter with Him is unforgettable.

Discipline is not difficult.

Discipline is not a dirty word, and it is not difficult. It is only as challenging as we allow it to be. Take a look at your life. Most of us have the same routine everyday. The same way that you train yourself to get up and brush your teeth, get dressed, and go to school or work, is the same way that you can absolutely discipline yourself to spend time with God. If you see it as a chore, it will be a chore. If you see it as intimate fellowship, it will be that.

Create an environment conducive to greeting Him in the Word and in worship (adoration), and I guarantee you that if you put your all into it for even 30 days, your entire life will shift. You will go from struggling to fill up an hour to being completely lost in Him. It really is all up to you. Remember how important it is that you deploy. Think about how He longs for you, and don't let yourself rob Him of that time. And you know what? If you are struggling with wanting to give Him that time, show up to tell Him that too, and watch Him work. He cares about you deeply. I cannot stress that enough. He wants the best for you, and He wants to deploy you so that the world can see His glory. He wants to end your suffering and answer your questions. He does not want a visitation. He wants to dwell with you. Move Him in. It will be the best thing you ever do.

Warrior Deploy!

After all that we have shared, you know how important it is for you to draw close to Him—to take residence in His presence, so that you can receive your rightful identity, and take your rightful place in the earth. It is time for you to collect your rightful inheritance and live from the abundance of the supernatural.

Don't let your concern for who and where you are today keep you from the throne. It is always the perfect time to step in. I recall a man at the pool of Bethesda. Some 30+ years he sat waiting for someone to help into the pool so that he could be healed. Jesus seeing how out of alignment his condition was with the will of the Father asks him if he wants to be made whole, and He heals him. His need was not for the kindness of man to take pity on him. His need was for a supernatural encounter with eternity that would set him free from more than just blindness. He got up whole.

It's time for you to be made whole by stepping into all God says you are. Anything that you don't move to conquer will inadvertently conquer you. Not knowing who you fully are beyond a title will conquer you.

Aren't you tired of life as you know it? Aren't you fed up with not seeing the power of God moving in your life and all around you? Aren't you tired of not seeing your prayers answered and of not experiencing the abundance we keep hearing of?

Get up! Go after your more. Go after God with all you have. Fall into Him and stay right there and watch Him redeem the time. Shake off what so easily besets you and run into the more excellent way. Ask the Holy Spirit to lead you into all truth. Ask God who you are and why you exist. Be persistent in your quest and your thirst for Him, and you will find that you are one of the most powerful forces in the earth that the enemy has to contend with.

Psalm 91 is your portion and your promise.

He that dwelleth in the secret place of the most High shall abide under the shadow of the Almighty. Psalm 91:1 KJV

The term "secret place" is a common expression for bedchamber. It's a place of intimacy. When a woman entered the bedchamber of her husband, it was to consummate their vows. And as she did so, her expectation was that she would conceive.

As you make your dwelling place in Him, as you enter the place of intimacy with, you shall live peacefully under His shadow. That is the assurance that there is nowhere that you can you can go that His presence will not be with you. As you enter the secret chamber, and as often as you do, you can expect a deposit to be made in you that you can birth out into the earth! There is no limit to His divine consummation. Get all you can get.

Every promise made in this chapter thereafter is God reminding you that what He has deposited in you and released you to deploy will not and cannot be destroyed. The psalmist sings a divine extreme that describes God's all powerful Hand and relentless will to protect what you carry. You can walk through warfare in the heat of the battle and not a bullet shall touch you. Many may fall but you will stand, the angels shall deploy to keep your footing. No evil shall befall you and not a plague will come near your doorstep!

Come on! Let the promise ring out in your soul. If you call He will answer. He'll be with you in your troubles and with long life He will satisfy you.

Your reward for making Him your dwelling place is Him! We should not be apathetic to that. If we knew who He was for real we would run swiftly after Him. He is the prize. There is no part of Him you will not have. When you have Him you have everything. Let yourself see yourself in that place. Let yourself imagine that kind of protection. Let yourself feel that kind of love washing over you. And know that when you go, you will never go alone.

Remember we said earlier that every form of deployment matters. *"so shall* My word *be that goeth forth out of My mouth: It* shall not return *unto Me* void, *but it shall accomplish that which I please, and it shall prosper in the thing."* Isaiah 55:11.

We have talked about the authority at our disposal, and we have shared that it gives us legal jurisdiction to act on behalf of the Father to execute His will over every demonic illegality at any given time. THAT is the summation of being an authentic worshipper. Miracles, signs, and wonders shall follow you if apply this information to your life. However, everyone is not dead. We have a responsibility to the living. Everyone is not sick. We have a responsibility to the well. Everyone is not blind. We have a responsibility to the seeing. Everybody is not deaf. We have a responsibility to the hearing.

We are not ascending into Him solely for the operation in and execution of power. We are ascending into Him because we have an obligation to respond to God's divine intention. There are no limitations in Him. We want everything God wants, however He wants it.

This entire book has revealed that **relationship** must be our highest priority above all else. Pursue it relentlessly and watch the power of God invade your very existence and deploy you into pulling Eternity down into time. Get ready for the miraculous supernatural life you were always destined to have.

Closing Prayer

God, our Sovereign,

I thank you for these readers who have now been exposed to the principles of Kingdom and deployment. Through this work that you have anointed and chosen me to write, I know that many lives will change as a result of hearing the Word and then doing it.

We need further revelation and information from you, and commit ourselves today to our awakening, our arising, and our shining.

We understand that you have created us for a purpose, and it is our desire to fulfill that purpose. Whatever barriers stand in our way, we release them to you—those we know about and those we don't. We submit ourselves to you again, asking you to reveal to us who we really are and why we exist.

As you release that information, we will be careful to walk with you through the process of understanding, renewing our minds, healing, transforming, shifting, growing, and giving.

You are indeed a faithful and Holy God. We come to you not out of fear and duty, but out of obligation to be the living Word you intended us to be so that Your will can be done on earth as you laid it all out in Heaven.

We are imperfect, and maybe at times we are rebellious or simply afraid, but if we have learned anything through this study you have put in our hands, it is that our lives do not belong to us. We willingly turn ourselves back over to you, and trust what you decide. We will even go forth if we feel afraid, because you have assured us that you will be with us always, and in this work you have pointed out our authority and our citizenship rights.

Thank you for loving and choosing us. Thank you for steering and guiding us. Thank you for calling us forth to be examples of your character, love, and your light. Give us the strength to endure the corrections, the changes, and the process. Give us the courage to face ourselves where we fall short, and the desire and will to change and grow.

We choose to delight ourselves in you and to accept what you ultimately desire for us, knowing that your plan is greater and glorious. Make us willing and ready to be deployed! We say amen, which we know means, "It shall be so."

ABOUT THE AUTHOR

Heireina Patrei Wallace, affectionately known as "Rein" or "Lady Rein" in art, ministry, and authorship, was born and raised in San Francisco, CA to Huey P Johnson and Evangelist Yuvetta Pryor. Her father, prior to his passing, prophesied over her in the womb indicating that she would be a dynamic and anointed woman of God carrying on his legacy of high profile ministry and profound commitment to the cause of Christ, and that she would be used to bring deliverance and healing to the nations.

Rein was saved, anointed, and called to preach at the tender age of seven-- a ministry prodigy often astounding those who heard her preach with her keen insight, revelation, and theological reflections on the word. Her ministry was developed in the Church of God in Christ, where she held many positions in ministry respectively, including: youth and young adult leader and minister, praise and worship leader, preacher, children's ministries leader, Sunday school and Bible study teacher, church administrator, drama ministries coordinator, praise dance ministries leader, etc.

Called to pursue advancement in ministry, Rein was later licensed as a Reverend in the A.M.E church prior to a call to leaving it to support her pastor in launching a non-denominational ministry geared toward reaching the marginalized and oppressed. It was there that she continued her work in the ministry serving as a clergy member, minister of music, and youth and children's leader while launching out as an independent and highly sought after inspirational artist. Her ministry in the music has enabled her to minister alongside gospel greats and has afforded her numerous accolades throughout the bay area and beyond.

While Rein grew up fully committed to ministry in every aspect, her young life outside of the church was a devastating one that included early prostitution by her grandmother, molestation, rape, abortion, and violence. Her passion increased for the people of God, especially for those with past traumatic and abusive experiences who needed support and ministry to their deeper needs and weren't being ministered to in the church. Fully persuaded that she could be used to minister to the hurting, marginalized, and oppressed, she began to seek God for the role that she could play in encouraging and promoting healing and transformation. In 2010, God ushered her off of a lucrative job as a Human Resources Executive and Chief Administrator and compelled her to chronicle her life's journey toward transformation in her book, "I Am Not Garbage." From there, God has opened numerous doors for her and established several partnerships that allow her to minister the gospel of transformation and the Word in general to multiple youth and women's organizations, social clubs, schools, and churches.

Today, Rein spends her time in servitude to Christ through full time ministry, and after joining in holy matrimony has become Prophetess and Co-Pastor alongside her husband Apostle Derrick Wallace for Greater Deliverance Global Ministries based in Atlanta, GA with churches also planted in California, Africa, Asia, and the Middle East.

Prophetess Rein is a dynamic praise and worship leader, an author, a youth, family, and parent coach, a life coach, a spiritual coach, a mentor, and a highly sought after motivational speaker, Revivalist, Prophetess, and preacher who is committed to leading others in the direction of wholeness, transformation, and freedom through the work of her organization Transformation University, Her "Say Something Campaign," a campaign that encourages others to put voice to their pain with the end goal of healing and transformation, and through her "Virtual Transformation Training Center," an online mentoring and membership program.

Rein reaches many through transparent testimony, speaking engagements, classes, webinars, music, devotionals, books, social and other media as a means of drawing others into their complete wholeness and transformation—teaching principles of living healthy and wholesome lives free from the pain of the past. She is also the proud mother of three beautiful boys, Paris, Pierre, and Caleb-Lyric, and one adopted daughter LaRaya Rodgers.

Contact
Email: bookprophetressrein@gmail.com
Website: www.reininternational.com

Social Media
Facebook: www.facebook.com/reininternational
Instagram: www.instagram.com/reininternational
Twitter: www.twitter.com/prophetessrein

Bookstore Link:
https://transform-with-rein.myshopify.com

Podcast Link:
www.reininternational.com/podcast

Made in the USA
Middletown, DE
30 September 2020

20853871R00158